Ancient CONTEXT
Ancient FAITH

JESUS
AND THE JEWISH
FESTIVALS

Uncover the Ancient Culture, Discover Hidden Meanings.

GARY M. BURGE

ZONDERVAN®

ZONDERVAN.com/
AUTHORTRACKER
follow your favorite authors

ZONDERVAN

Jesus and the Jewish Festivals
Copyright © 2012 by Gary M. Burge

This title is also available as a Zondervan ebook.
Visit www.zondervan.com/ebooks.

Requests for information should be addressed to:

Zondervan, *Grand Rapids, Michigan 49530*

Library of Congress Cataloging-in-Publication Data

Burge, Gary M. 1952
       Jesus and the Jewish festivals / Gary M. Burge.
          p. cm. — (Ancient context, ancient faith)
       Includes bibliographical references. (pp. 137 – 39)
       ISBN 978-0-310-28047-7 (softcover)
       1. Jesus Christ — Person and offices. 2. Fast and feasts — Judaism. 3. Fasts and
feast in the Bible. 4. Bible. N.T. — Criticism, interpretation, etc I. Title.
       BT205.B88 2011
       232.9'5 — dc23   2011038044

Cover and Interior Design: Kirk Douponce, DogEared Design
Cover photography: © Hanan Isachar/Alamy
Printed in China

13 14 15 16 17 18 /CTC/ 21 20 19 18 17 16 15 14 13 12 11 10 9 8 7 6 5 4 3 2

For Grace Elizabeth

CONTENTS

ANCIENT CONTEXT, ANCIENT FAITH

EVERY COMMUNITY of Christians throughout history has framed its understanding of spiritual life within the context of its own culture. Byzantine Christians living in the fifth century and Puritan Christians living over a thousand years later used the world in which they lived to work out the principles of Christian faith, life, and identity. The reflex to build house churches, monastic communities, medieval cathedrals, steeple-graced village-centered churches, or auditoriums with theater seating will always spring from the dominant cultural forces around us.

Even the way we understand "faith in Christ" to some degree is shaped by these cultural forces. For instance, in the last three hundred years, Western Christians have abandoned seeing faith as a chiefly communal exercise (although this is not true in Africa or Asia). Among the many endowments of the European Enlightenment, individualism reigns supreme: Christian faith is a personal, private endeavor. We prefer to say, "*I have accepted Christ*," rather than define ourselves through a *community* that follows Christ. Likewise (again, thanks to the Enlightenment), we have elevated rationalism as a premier value. Among many Christians faith is a construct of the mind, an effort at knowledge gained through study, an assent to a set of theological propositions. Sometimes even knowing *what you believe* trumps belief itself.

To be sure, many Christians today are challenging these Enlightenment assumptions and are seeking to chart a new path. Nevertheless the new path charted is as much a by-product of modern cultural trends as any other. For example, we live today in a highly therapeutic society. Even if we are unaware of the discipline of psychology, we are still being shaped by values it has brought to our culture over the last hundred years. Faith today has an emotional, feeling-centered basis. Worship is measured by the emotive responses and the heart. "Felt needs" of a congregation shape many sermons.

Therefore, defining Christian faith as a personal choice based on well-informed convictions and inspired by emotionally engaging worship is a formula for spiritual formation that may be natural to us — but it may have elements that are foreign to the experience of other Christians in other cultures or other centuries. I imagine that fifth-century Christians would feel utterly lost in a modern church with its worship band and theater seating where lighting, sound, refreshments, and visual media are closely monitored. They might wonder if this *modern church* was chiefly indebted to entertainment, like a tamed, baptized version of Rome's public arenas. They might also wonder how 10,000 people can gain any sense of shared life or community when each family comes and goes by car, lives long distances away, and barely recognizes the person sitting next to them.

THE ANCIENT LANDSCAPE

If it is true that *every* culture provides a framework in which the spiritual life is understood, the same must be said about the ancient world. The setting of Jesus and Paul in the Roman Empire was likewise shaped by cultural forces quite different than our own. If we fail to understand these cultural forces, we will fail to understand many of the things Jesus and Paul taught.

This does not mean that the culture of the biblical world enjoys some sort of divine approval or endorsement. We do not need to imitate the biblical world in order to live a more biblical life. This was a culture that had its own preferences for dress, speech, diet, music, intellectual thought, religious expression, and personal identity. And their cultural values were no more significant than are our own. Modesty in antiquity was expressed in a way we may not understand. The arrangement of marriage partners would be foreign to our world of personal dating. Even how one prays (seated or standing, arms upraised or folded, aloud or silent) has norms dictated by culture.

But if this is true—if cultural values are presupposed within every faithful community, both now and two thousand years ago—then the stories we read in the Bible may presuppose themes that are completely obscure to us. Moreover, when we read the Bible, we may misrepresent its message because we simply do not understand the cultural instincts of the first century. We live two thousand years distant; we live in the West and the ancient Middle East is not native territory for us.

INTERPRETING FROM AFAR

This means we need to be cautious interpreters of the Bible. We need to be careful lest we presuppose that *our cultural instincts* are the same as those represented in the Bible. We need to be *culturally aware* of our own place in time—and we need to work to comprehend the cultural context of the Scriptures that we wish to understand. Too often interpreters have lacked cultural awareness when reading the Scriptures. We have failed to recognize the gulf that exists between who we are today and the context of the Bible. We have forgotten that we read the Bible as foreigners, as visitors who have traveled not only to a new geography but a new century. We are literary tourists who are deeply in need of a guide.

The goal of this series is to be such a guide—to explore themes from the biblical world that are often misunderstood. In what sense, for instance, did the physical geography of Israel shape its people's sense of spirituality? How did the storytelling of Jesus presuppose cultural themes now lost to us? What celebrations did Jesus know intimately (such as a child's birth, a wedding, or a burial)? What agricultural or religious festivals did he attend? How did he use common images of labor or village life or social hierarchy when he taught? Did he use humor or allude to politics? In many cases — just as in our world — the more delicate matters are handled indirectly and it takes expert guidance to revisit their correct meaning.

In a word, this series employs *cultural anthropology, archaeology, and contextual backgrounds* to open up new vistas for the Christian reader. If the average reader suddenly sees a story or an idea in a new way, if a familiar passage is suddenly opened for new meaning and application, this effort has succeeded.

I am indebted to many experiences and people who awakened my sense of urgency about this interpretive method. My first encounter came as a student at Beirut's *Near East School of Theology* in the 1970s. Since then scholars such as David Daube, J. D. M. Derrett, S. Safrai, M. Stern, E. P. Sanders, Charles Kraft, James Strange, Kenneth Bailey, Bruce Malina, I. Howard Marshall, and a host of others have contributed to how I read the New Testament. Bailey's many books in particular as well as his long friendship have been prominent in inspiring my efforts into the cultural anthropology of the ancient world. In addition I have been welcomed many times by the Arabic-speaking church in Lebanon, Syria, Iraq, Jordan, Palestine, and Egypt and there became attuned to the way that cultural setting influences how we read texts. To them and their great and historic faith, I owe a considerable debt.

Finally, special thanks are due to Katya Covrett and Verlyn Verbrugge at Zondervan. Verlyn's expert editing and Katya's creativity improved the book enormously. In addition Kim Tanner at Zondervan worked as senior visual content editor. Her skill at finding the unusual, arresting photos within huge archives never ceases to amaze me. Thanks are also due to Megan LaRusso, my research assistant, whose keen eye corrected mistakes that everyone else missed.

Gary M. Burge
Wheaton, Illinois

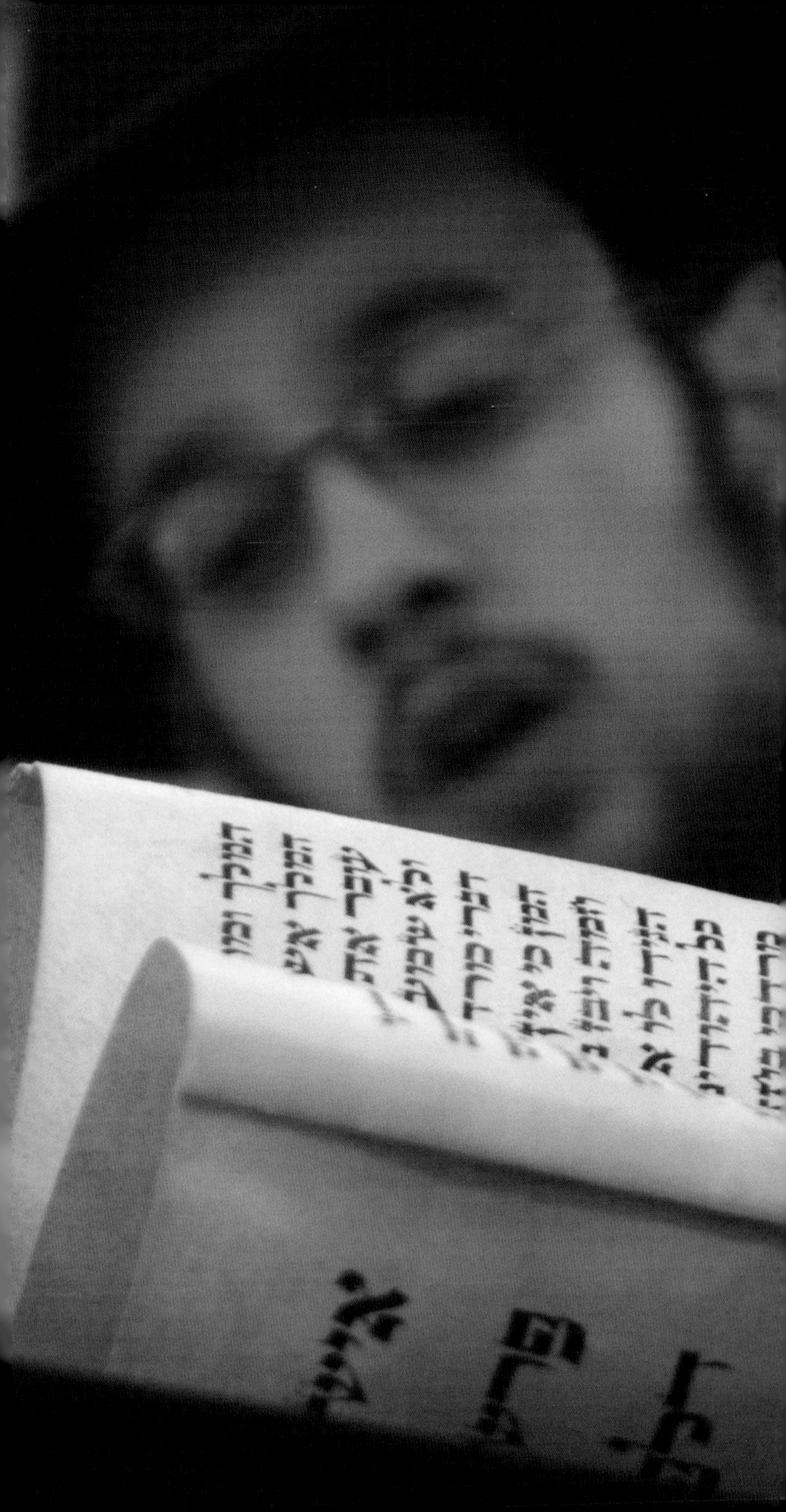

Chapter 1

THE FESTIVALS OF JUDAISM

EVERYONE ENJOYS public festivals and holidays. Through them we tell stories that are sacred to our shared histories, or we simply enjoy remembering the seasons in which we live. Festivals are also closely tied to culture. Long-practiced customs take on subtle symbols that are barely noticed by an outsider.

If you live in England, for example, you simply must know what Guy Fawkes Day means — and join the bonfire that night (November 5). Here's the backstory: in November 1605 a man named Guy Fawkes decided to blow up Parliament and the House of Lords, kill King James I, and restore Catholicism to Britain. He failed. The "Gunpowder Plot" and its demise (Fawkes was caught guarding barrels of gunpowder in the basement of Parliament) was soon a celebration, and it evolved into a British holiday with Fawkes annually being burned in effigy over huge bonfires in almost every English city. The night ends with fireworks, carnivals, and celebrations.

In Scandinavia, particularly Sweden, the Saint Lucia Festival occurs on December 13. While not a national holiday, "Santa Lucia" is firmly held by the culture. A young girl is

PEOPLE CELEBRATING GUY FAWKES DAY
WITH A BONFIRE

chosen to lead an entourage of other girls in a public procession
(often from a church). The young "Lucia" wears white robes,
a red sash, and a crown of lighted candles while distributing
cookies (usually *pepparkakor* or gingersnaps). The origin of
this festival goes back to a young Sicilian woman who lived in
about AD 300 and died as a martyr under the Roman Emperor
Diocletian. Numerous legends evolved over time about how she

YOUNG GIRLS CELEBRATING
THE SANTA LUCIA FESTIVAL

used candles in Rome's dark catacombs to bring food and aid to hiding Christians. Today in Sweden you'll be served *Lussekatt*, a bun made with saffron—and if you're in high school, you probably spent the entire previous night carousing about your town ("*Lusse-vigil*"). Today Lucia is closely linked to Christmas celebrations, but few Swedes can really tell you where it all came from.

FESTIVALS AND CULTURAL CODES

We have similar festivals in the United States. Some are well-known (Christmas, Easter, Thanksgiving) while others are now more obscure (St. Patrick's Day, Labor Day). Sometimes we barely remember the historical origins of our festivals. In the United States Halloween has clear guidelines for what we're supposed to do. But few recall why we do it or know the link to the church festival of "All Saints' Day." We celebrate the holiday and we don't understand it fully.

Festivals also have symbols that everyone may recognize but are difficult to explain. We know that the colors green and red belong to Christmas; black and orange go with Halloween. And pastels belong to Easter. These codes have a public consensus. In America no one would set out black and orange Easter eggs. But other codes are less clear. Imagine explaining to someone from rural western China all of the symbols of Christmas: wreaths, holly, Santa (and his outfit), mistletoe, plus all of the religious imagery: the manger, the star, baby Jesus, and endless presents. I'm not sure if I could explain how mistletoe and the Bethlehem star go together.

But we handle all of this with ease, and a part of the enjoyment is reliving the numer-

NATIVITY SETS ARE COMMON CHRISTMAS DECORATIONS IN THE WESTERN WORLD.

ous memories that come from the festival's events. Occasionally some of these codes are so subtle that only a cultural insider would understand. I once asked a class of students to find me the most obscure symbol that immediately brought to mind "Easter." Their answer: marshmallow Peeps. If you're unsure what there are, there is an entire website devoted to them.[1]

However, some societies are comprehensively religious, and in these places national holidays and religious festivals run together. The Muslim celebration of Ramadan comes to mind. Ramadan is the ninth month on the Arabic calendar. In the ancient world it was a time in Arabia desperate for relief from the heat and without abundant water and food. Daytime fasting for this one month became common. The birth of Islam in the seventh century made Ramadan fasting official. For one month Muslims will fast from sunset to sundown (this is stipulated in the Qur'an, 2:183 – 187) and then feast in the evening.

In places like Egypt, streets are decorated with elaborate awnings where public dinners are enjoyed. Often the daily fast is broken with dates — a common Arabian food (used by Muhammad to break his own Ramadan fasts). The month of Ramadan ends with the grand feast of *Eid* (*Eid ul-Fitr*) filled with traditional foods dictated by each region. Generally a

FATTOUSH, A MEAL EATEN IN CELEBRATION OF RAMADAN

sheep, camel, or goat is sacrificed for the feast. But to outsiders, this is as opaque as Christmas is to Chinese Buddhists. If you don't know how to eat *fattoush* or if you don't like lamb *mansef* with *laban*, you've never celebrated Ramadan in Jordan or Syria or Lebanon.

A PLASTIC SANTA REPRESENTS CHRISTMAS TO MANY.

It is not surprising that outsiders get confused in festivals that belong to other cultures. Once I was in the huge *Khan el Khalili* market of Cairo where I saw a Muslim man selling tall inflatable plastic Santas. I asked him, "What does this red fat man mean?" "I don't know," he said. "But I think Americans use these to decorate their homes." I didn't have the heart to straighten him out.

RELIGIOUS FESTIVALS IN ANTIQUITY

If it is true that our communities enjoy their peculiar festivals, the same was true of people living two thousand years ago. We have evidence from countless literary records that festivals were everywhere. And in some respects they share a few motifs with our own. They were keenly aware of the agricultural calendar; thus, in the northern hemisphere both fall and spring were important to celebrate the end of the summer harvest or the beginning of spring, when new life appears. Ancient people also were alert to the shortening of days and could mark the fall and spring equinox when day and night were equal. The "loss of light" in the autumn climaxed with midwinter (or the winter

JULIUS CAESAR

THE ROMAN GOD JANUS

solstice), and here festivals might celebrate light and pray for the return of longer days.

Most ancient calendars were also lunar; that is, they followed the phases of the moon. This rhythm was easy to measure, but today we barely notice. A new moon was followed by a crescent (the lunar phases move horizontally across the face of the moon from right to left), and this led to a full quarter and finally a full moon. Then the moon began to disappear (following these same phases in reverse). This cycle took about a month and was the basis of both the earliest Roman and Jewish calendars. The solar annual calendar that divides a year into twelve months of thirty or thirty-one days, which we use today, was introduced by Julius Caesar (100–44 BC). By the time of Augustus (63 BC–AD 14) it was the common imperial calendar. Many of the month names we use today come from Rome. July stems from "Julius" (think: Julius Caesar). January (or Januarius) owes its name to the Roman god Janus (god of gates, doors [Latin: *ianus*], and harvests).

The passing of time and the publishing of calendars helped

above all to orchestrate the many religious festivals that both Romans and Jews celebrated. The Roman months held many of these that we do not recognize today. For instance, March 1 and 14 held festivals for Mars, god of war. April held the promise of spring and so the Feast of Parilia on April 21 evolved from a day to bless the sheep to a celebration of Rome's founding. Floralia on April 28 was a fertility festival that invoked the gods to bring rich harvests and flocks in the new season. On August 12, you would sacrifice to Hercules. In each case, ceremonies, foods, songs, and a pause in the normal routine of life were expected.

The Romans exported their calendar and their many religious ceremonies throughout the empire—including Judea. We can find evidence of this in the most remote areas imaginable. For example, on the far northern boundary of Syria along the Euphrates River there was a Roman outpost called Dura Europas. In the 1920s British soldiers discovered the long lost town beneath sand. It was then excavated, and in 1932 archaeologists discovered the Jewish synagogue of the community dating to the early third century AD. Its wall paintings were intact, and today they can be seen in the National Museum of Damascus. But also found was a small scroll in Latin giving a list of religious festivals that ought to be observed. No doubt Roman sol-

© Christine Osborne Pictures/Alamy

THE DURA EUROPAS SYNAGOGUE

ONE OF THE MANY PAINTINGS
WITHIN THE DURA EUROPAS

diers far from home wanted to plan their holidays. It was a remarkable find and gave us insight into how widely Roman religious life was practiced.

In culturally cohesive and strong nations within the Roman Empire, the Roman festival calendar had to compete with local customs that would not budge. And Judea (or Israel) was one such example. Here the Romans met an ancient people whose religious traditions were well-developed, filled with rich festivals, anchored to a temple, and needed no Roman additions. The Jewish commitment to worshiping one God, the God of Israel, left little room for supplemental festivals that might give honor or recognition to Hercules or Zeus. In fact, since Judaism did not take kindly to its Roman occupation, resisting these "foreign" religious traditions was a sign of patriotism and zeal for things Jewish.

Jerusalem (even under its occupation) did not host a *Roman* temple (unlike most cities in the empire). When a Roman freighter or warship tied up at Caesarea Maritima (Judea's Mediterranean port), a fabulous temple dedicated to Augustus stood over the wharf. But as soon as you traveled east into the

JESUS AND THE JEWISH FESTIVALS

hills toward Jerusalem, most signs of Roman religion vanished, and soon the magnificent Jewish temple of Herod the Great came into view. Here was a city utterly devoted to its own religious traditions and its complete commitment to the God of Israel.

It was only in AD 135, when Jerusalem was totally destroyed, its

HERCULES FIGHTING WITH CENTAUR NESSUS

people expelled, and the city renamed Aelia Capitolina by the

NOTHING REMAINS OF THE TEMPLE OF AUGUSTUS AT CAESAREA MARITIMA. IT USED TO BE LOCATED ALONG THE SKYLINE OF THIS PHOTO.

Romans, that a temple to Jupiter was built on the site of the Jewish temple.

JEWISH RELIGIOUS FESTIVALS

In ancient Judea national and religious ceremonies were one and the same. There were no "secular holidays" since all history and politics were considered an extension of Israel's religious life. We probably have never experienced anything like this. Because of our pluralism, our culture does not have a "grand religious story" that we celebrate together. Today we would need to travel to Israel or a Muslim country such as Egypt to see how this might work.

The most important feast in the Jewish calendar happened each week. It was the "Sabbath" — a term taken from the Greek (*sabbaton*), which in turn came from the Hebrew word for "cease" (*shabat*). Because God ceased work on the seventh day of creation (Gen. 2:1 – 3), so too his people were required to rest; this was codified in the Ten Commandments (Ex. 20:8 – 11). "Remember the Sabbath day to keep it holy." Since the Jewish "day" began at sundown, Sabbath began on Friday evening at dusk and continued to Saturday dusk. All work had to cease as Jews met together (later in synagogues) to punctuate the end of their work week with prayer, study, and rest.

By Jesus' day, religious parties exercised tremendous effort in debating what qualified as prohibited work. As we will see, Jesus disagreed with many of their decisions. Nevertheless, Sabbath observance became a hallmark of Jewish identity in the Roman world. Some Romans admired Jews for it (Josephus, *Ag. Ap.* 2.40), while others resented it (*Ag. Ap.* 2.20).

The annual festivals of Judaism were built around three great agricultural feasts (see Ex. 23:14 – 17; Deut. 16:1 – 15), which by the era of Jesus involved pilgrimages to the great city of Jerusalem. Three pilgrimage festivals were mandated in Exodus 23:14 – 17: a seven-day springtime festival centered around the cereal harvest; an early summer festival when cereal harvests were done; and an autumn festival of ingathering, when olives, grapes, and other fruits were harvested (cf. Ex. 34:18 – 23).

Judaism's Annual Pilgrimage Feasts

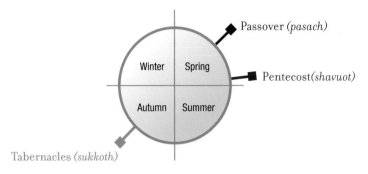

Judaism was an agricultural culture that cherished its abundant crops. A writing called *The Letter of Aristeas* describes the zeal of Jewish farmers:

> . . . *their land is thickly covered with large numbers of olive trees and cereal crops . . . vines and abundant honey. As for the fruit trees and date palms which they have, no number can be given. They have many flocks and herds of various kinds. . . . So they perceived the areas that need to be populated and designed cities and villages accordingly. (Aristeas 112 – 13)[2]*

In many respects, the Sabbath cycle of seven influenced the three annual celebrations as perhaps the premier model of what a festival should be. One feast might follow another by "seven" weeks; and a stay in Jerusalem might last "seven" days. Sabbath was the key festival; agricultural feasts were an ongoing expression of it.

Did everyone travel to Jerusalem three times per year? We doubt it. Otherwise entire Galilee villages would have been vacant. It is more likely that many traveled to these festivals but also that many stayed back.

In each of the annual feasts, Israel merged two important traditions: agricultural thanksgiving and the recitation of its sacred history. Woven through its ceremonies were opportunities not merely to express gratefulness to God but also to rehearse what God had done on Israel's behalf. As we might expect of every national festival throughout history, there were symbols and codes that people enjoyed.

But here is the critical part for us today: in order to understand how Jesus responded to his own festival culture, we must

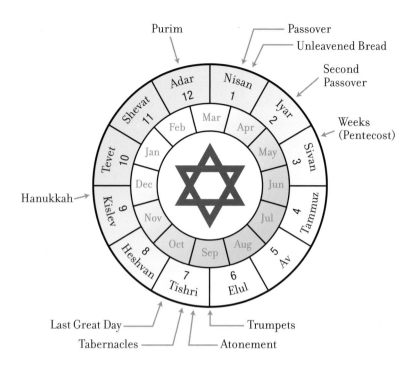

have some understanding of the traditions at work in his era. Judaism had its own calendar and named its months. Its religious or ceremonial "new year" (distinct from Rosh Hashanah, the civil new year) began in spring with the first month called Nisan.

In the spring (on the Jewish date Nisan 14) Israel recognized new life emerging as a gift from God. Ancient tribal Israel (before the exodus) had always celebrated the growth of flocks with a sacrificial feast (see Ex. 5:1). This was soon joined by a celebration of the incoming cereal harvest (particularly the barley harvest). Shepherds and farmers together could then praise God with a seven-day ceremonial feast in Jerusalem called Passover (Heb. *Pesach*).

Although only men were required to attend the ceremonies (and great debate attended defining who qualified as a required male), in Jesus' day Jewish families would commonly travel to Jerusalem with their sacrifices and ordinarily remain there for seven days, until Nisan 22. No work could be done during the feast (another parallel to Sabbath), and we can expect that the days were filled with song, hearty eating, storytelling, dance, and opportunities to visit with old friends. The week ended with the formal "waving of sheaf" (a bit of wheat

ANCIENT TRIBAL ISRAEL HAD ALWAYS
CELEBRATED THE GROWTH OF FLOCKS
WITH A SACRIFICIAL FEAST. HERE SAMARITANS
CELEBRATE THEIR PASSOVER SACRIFICE.

or barley) anticipating the harvest to come (Lev. 23:10 – 14).
The book of Deuteronomy strictly prohibited the celebration
of Passover anywhere but "the place the LORD will choose as
a dwelling for his Name" (Deut. 16:2; i.e., Jerusalem), and it
wasn't until after the destruction of Jerusalem that domestic
Passover celebrations became common.

BARLEY WAS AN IMPORTANT PART OF
THE CEREAL HARVEST.

SUKKOTH BOOTH

The second great festival occurred seven weeks after the end of the Passover festival (Lev. 23:15). If Passover marked the beginning of the cereal harvest, seven weeks later, the end of that harvest was at hand. This festival in Greek was called Pentecost (Heb. *Shavuot*). The great summer drought was now beginning when tilling the soil was nearly impossible. Yet stores of grain were collected and were ready for sifting and milling. Another pilgrimage to the Jerusalem temple now brought the fruit of this harvest as a thanksgiving offering to God.

THE FESTIVAL OF TABERNACLES RECALLED THE HARVESTING OF FIGS, POMEGRANATES, GRAPES, AND OLIVES.

The third pilgrimage festival took place in the autumn during the seventh month of the Jewish year (Lev. 23:33–44). This is called Tabernacles (Heb. *Sukkoth*). The term refers to a rough shelter (Heb. *sukkah*) made out of branches, and it recalled the harvesting of tree and vine (figs, pomegranates, grapes, or olives). Such crops were so valuable that farmers would often stay in their fields to protect them. Even today, such harvest shelters can be seen throughout the Arab countryside in Palestine since the custom has not changed. This was a time of joy and celebration since it was truly the end of the harvest year.

These were the three great festivals of the Jewish year: Passover (*Pesach*), Pentecost (*Shavuot*), and Tabernacles (*Sukkoth*). But in addition to celebrating the agricultural year, these three festivals became opportunities to celebrate the great stories of Israel's experiences with God. They formed a cycle that would retell this great drama and pull important lessons from it. Passover retold the story of the exodus from Egypt under Moses' leadership. Pentecost remembered the covenant given at Mount Sinai after Israel had spent three months in the desert. Finally, Tabernacles recalled the wilderness wanderings (after departing Mount Sinai), when Israel had to live in temporary shelters.

Baker Photo Archive

TABERNACLE SHELTERS USED FOR PROTECTING OLIVE TREES REMINDED THE ISRAELITE OF DESERT SHELTERS USED EARLIER DURING ISRAEL'S GREAT DESERT JOURNEY TO THE PROMISED LAND.

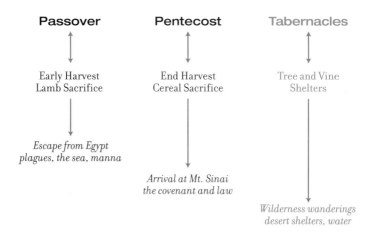

Passover	Pentecost	Tabernacles
Early Harvest Lamb Sacrifice	End Harvest Cereal Sacrifice	Tree and Vine Shelters
Escape from Egypt *plagues, the sea, manna*	*Arrival at Mt. Sinai* *the covenant and law*	*Wilderness wanderings* *desert shelters, water*

Within each of these agricultural festivals, links could be found to the sacred story so that it all could be presented together. For instance, a sacrificed lamb saved the Israelites in Egypt from the tenth plague, and it was such a lamb that was sacrificed in the springtime as a thanksgiving to God for the growth of flocks. Tabernacle shelters used for protecting olive trees reminded the Israelite of desert shelters used earlier during Israel's great desert journey to the Promised Land.

JESUS AND THE JEWISH FESTIVALS

When we think about the Gospels and the life of Jesus, we must assume that he knew these festivals well and celebrated them regularly. Occasionally the Bible gives us a hint that a minor festival is going on. For instance, near Passover Jews celebrated the feast of Purim, which retold the story of Esther and her courageous defense of her Jewish people in Persia. Because of a plot to kill the Jews, Esther approached the king of Persia during a banquet and was asked to make a request. "Even up to half the kingdom, it will be given you," said the king (Esth. 5:3; 7:2).

In another curious banquet, this time in the Gospels, we learn that Herod Antipas of Galilee was hosting a banquet (near his birthday). Here too when a young woman pleases Herod, he asks her, "Whatever you ask I will give you, *up to half my kingdom*" (Mark 6:23, emphasis added). In an ironic turn, John the Baptist is killed (rather than Haman, the Persian enemy of the Jews). The heroism of Esther is perfectly turned upside down and we wonder—was this a Purim banquet at Herod's Galilee palace?

On other occasions we know that Jesus held the major festivals in highest respect. *He was an observant Jew.* He recognized and observed the Sabbath. He traveled to Jerusalem for Passover and Tabernacles. And we can easily assume that he was intimately acquainted with the traditions of these festivals. In fact, the Gospels tell us that Jesus made use of these festivals in order to reveal remarkable things about himself.

This is where the stories become particularly interesting. *If we understand these festivals and their symbolism, then suddenly we understand the more profound things about Jesus and his work.* It would be as if a modern-day speaker decided—during Christmas season—to use the image of a Christmas tree to tell a story. Everyone in the audience would understand immediately what sort of tree this was and why perhaps a person might have it inside their home, or why it might be decorated. These ideas would be commonplace. *But if you lived outside our culture, grasping the finer elements of a Christmas tree story would be impossible.*

This, then, is our challenge. We want to probe those stories where Jesus appears at a Jewish festival, comprehend the hidden symbols and ideas at work there, and reflect on what Jesus is doing.

THE CHRISTMAS TREE IS OF LATE MEDIEVAL ORIGIN.

FAITH AND THE JEWISH FESTIVALS

I envy the discipline of the Jewish calendar cycle because it provides us with a different understanding of time. Here is what I mean. My own life has an annual rhythm that is dictated by a set of values that come entirely from the secular world: late summer is the beginning of school (and new clothes!), autumn brings Thanksgiving (and the Pilgrim story), Christmas is the "great festival" that has been almost entirely overwhelmed by consumerism and Santa. Easter is the celebration of spring. And summer is book-ended by Memorial Day and Labor Day. We also have a weekly festival: the weekend. Friday nights, Saturdays, and Sundays each have their own meanings dictated by the need for leisure. Even the dreaded "Monday morning" has its own set of coded responses. And who doesn't know what Black Friday means?[3]

Yet none of this speaks to the rhythms that I desire. In the Jewish cycle, the organizing center of the calendar is the mighty acts of God: Passover, Sinai, and the journey to the Promised Land. And within each cycle the story of salvation is retold. But in addition, Sabbath bears a uniquely *theological* meaning. We rest because God rested. Period. This is not time to visit Home Depot or Macy's. Marva Dawn has written *Keeping the Sabbath Wholly*,[4] which has transformed many of my friends'

© Johnny Stockshooter/Alamy

THE FIRST FULL MOON FOLLOWING THE SPRING EQUINOX MARKS THE BEGINNING OF PASSOVER.

thinking about Sunday. They've abandoned The American Weekend for something more profound and meaningful.

So I wonder: What would it mean to build a life with a genuine *theological* rhythm? A life that uses the Sabbath with real intentionality. I have known people who try to keep the seasons. One family I know has boxes and boxes of decorations for every holiday—including Valentine's and St. Patrick's Day. Their house

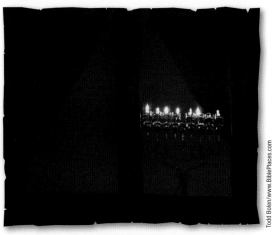

HANUKKAH CANDLES

SWEDISH CHRISTMAS CANDLES

looks a bit astonishing sometimes, particularly during Christmas. But it is not sentimentality that I want. *I desire a recital of what a season means as it is marked by a divine story.* This is perhaps one of the reasons I value attending a liturgical church. Here we mark the seasons (we *refuse* to sing Christmas carols during Advent—and the wise men are not permitted near the nativity scene until Epiphany) and watch as the liturgical colors change to indicate shifts in themes and stories. Sadly most evangelical churches have lost these rich theological symbols.

I remember once—early in spring—taking my night class up onto the roof of one of our academic buildings. We simply looked at the first full moon following the spring equinox. And I told them that Jews for thousands of years had marked this night, and tonight they were marking again the beginning of Passover. "This is the night Israel fled from Egypt." My students had nothing in their cultural vocabulary to compare with this. They were quiet and intrigued. They had now seen a calendar marker with a story.

I imagine children growing up with this. Instinctively they love the festivity of a changing theological season, and they never tire of their stories. I recall living for a few years in a Jewish Orthodox neighborhood in downtown Chicago. Hanukkah was about to begin, and all of the Jewish homes were putting beautiful Hanukkah candles in their bungalow bay windows. But our bay window was bare—until my eight-year-old daughter mounted a sizable Swedish Christmas candle setup prominently on the front window ledge. "Just so everyone knows," she announced. "We're celebrating Christmas here."

Chapter 2

JESUS AND THE SABBATH

John 5:1–47

THROUGHOUT THE Roman Empire, Jews were well-known for three distinguishing rituals: circumcision, Sabbath observance, and refusing to eat pork. Romans disliked circumcision (they thought of it as disfiguring), but they were intrigued by the Sabbath tradition. Some even imitated it by assuming a day free of work or copying Jewish Sabbath oil lamps.[5] Almost all pagan references to Jews make some note of the Sabbath.[6]

Jews counted their days from dusk to dusk (rather than midnight to midnight as we do). Therefore, Sabbath began at sundown on Friday evening and continued to sundown Saturday. On this one day each week, Jews abstained from work, they attended synagogue, and they shared in family meals, often joining with other Jewish families. The Hebrew word *Shabbat* is sometimes explained as coming from the word "seven" (Heb. *sheba^c^*). But it more likely stems from the verb *shabat*, which means "to cease." Work had to stop. This built a rest-rhythm into the Jewish "week" that continues with us today.

JUDAISM AND THE SABBATH

The Sabbath tradition is anchored first in the Old Testament.

MAN BLOWING THE *SHOFAR* NEAR THE WESTERN WALL

© PhotoStock-Israel/Alamy

God rested after six days of creation; he declared the seventh day holy and "rested from all his [creation] work" (Gen. 2:1–3). Israel observed this day of rest even before the giving of the law (Ex. 16:22–30), but the Sabbath was formally fixed in the Ten Commandments as the fourth rule to guide Israel's life (Ex. 20:8–11; Deut.

A WOMAN LIGHTING THE JEWISH SABBATH CANDLES

5:12–15). Sabbath observance was one of many tests of faithfulness to God and his laws (Neh. 9:14; Isa. 56:2–6).

By the New Testament era centuries of thoughtful discussion surrounded the Sabbath. It had evolved into a defining feature of faithful Jewish life. In a Jewish commentary on the book of Exodus from this era, the importance of the Sabbath is explained in terms of marriage:

> *Rabbi Simeon b. Yohai taught: Sabbath pleaded to the Holy One, blessed be he: "Everyone has a partner, while I have no partner!" God answered, "The community of Israel is your partner!" And then when Israel stood on Mt. Sinai, God said to them, "Remember what I said to the Sabbath that the community of Israel is your partner, as it is said, 'Remember the Sabbath day to keep it holy.'" (Ex. 20:8; Exodus Rabbah 11:8)[7]*

The first-century Jewish historian Josephus gives some suggestion how the Sabbath might begin. The synagogue *hazzan* (or leader) went to a high roof in his village and blew a

Z. Radovan/www.BibleLandPictures.com

shofar (or ram's horn) once to stop all work in the fields. A second time signaled all commercial activity should stop. And a third meant that household work must stop and the Sabbath candles should be lit (*J.W.* 4:582; Mishnah, Ḥullin 1:7). In Jerusalem this was done from

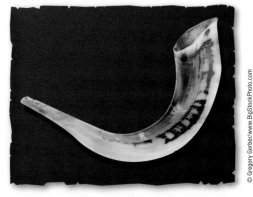

SHOFAR, A RAM'S HORN

a southern corner of the temple walls, alerting the entire city when Sabbath was near. Archaeologists have even discovered a marking stone from the top of the temple wall with an inscription telling the priest or Levite where to stand for blowing the *shofar*.

The main concern of Jewish law was how to observe this day of rest. The Old Testament gave few directions beyond "stay where [you] are" (Ex. 16:29), not building a fire (Ex. 35:3), not carrying things from place to place (Jer. 17:22), and ceasing

A FOURTH-CENTURY MOSAIC IN THE TIBERIAS
SYNAGOGUE DISPLAYS AN IMAGE OF A *SHOFAR*.

AN AREA NEAR THE SOUTHERN CORNER OF THE TEMPLE
WHERE THE LEADER WOULD BLOW THE *SHOFAR*

commercial or agricultural work (Neh. 13:15–22). But there were other questions. How far can I carry something without breaking Sabbath? May I lift a spoon to the table in order to set it? May I lift and move a chair to the table? And where is my "place" or domain that I cannot leave? If I cannot prepare food, may I cover it? May I heat it?

Soon countless rules were written, and it led one rabbi to comment that the rules for the Sabbath were "like a mountain hanging by a hair . . . the scriptures say little but the rules are many" (Mishnah, *Ḥagigah* 1:8).

The Jewish book of *Jubilees* was written about 150 BC; there we read how strict these rules could become. We learn that even God and his angels keep the Sabbath (*Jub.* 2.18, 30), and we are given the first list of rules that govern what could not be done (2.29–32; 50.6–13). For instance, the following were prohibited: preparing food, drawing water, riding an animal, having sex, sailing a boat, or building a fire. Intentional violations of Sabbath incurred the death penalty. Accidental violations required a special sin offering at the temple. It is hard to know how often these punishments were enforced or for that matter how someone judged their intentions.

The Mishnah is a compilation of Jewish laws written down

in about AD 200, but the volume contains many early rabbinic sayings that come from the first century. Here we find an entire tractate devoted to Sabbath. Guidance is given about how to light candles, how to heat food if a stove has residual heat, how to cover food, and even how to go outside. Chapter 7 is well-known because in it we find the thirty-nine classes of prohibited work. Among them: sowing, ploughing, baking, washing wool, making beds, sewing two stitches, pulling something down, building something up, striking a hammer, and carrying something from one domain to another.[8] Elsewhere we are told that we can clear crumbs from a table as long as the amount does not exceed the size of an olive. More than this and it is prohibited work.

A typical section concerns the tying of knots on Sabbath: "These are the knots for which they are accounted culpable [of breaking Sabbath]: camel-drivers' knots and sailors' knots; and as a man is culpable if he ties them — he is also culpable if he unties them. Rabbi Meir [about AD 140] says, 'You are not culpable if you tie a knot which can be untied with one hand' " (Mishnah, *Shabbat* 15:1). But 15:2 goes on to say that a woman may tie up an opening in her dress or the strings of her hair net or belt. A person can also tie up a sandal. Rabbi Eliezer ben Jacob [about AD 80] is quoted: "Cattle may be tied up before they stray away."

THE MISHNAH PROHIBITS THE TYING OR UNTYING OF CAMEL-DRIVERS' KNOTS AND SAILORS' KNOTS ON THE SABBATH.

Originally fighting in a war on the Sabbath was prohibited, but this led to devastating vulnerabilities. A Greek general Antiochus IV massacred many Jews by attacking on the Sabbath (1 Macc. 2:29–38; *Jub.* 50:12). This led to a decision that fighting *in self-defense* was acceptable on the Sabbath (1 Macc. 2:39–41).

But even this was a problem. The Roman general Pompey understood the Jewish rule when he laid siege to Jerusalem in 63 BC. On the Sabbath he built siege earthworks against the city's northern walls, which the Jews would not attack. He even moved battering rams (shipped from Tyre) right up to Jerusalem's gates on the Sabbath without a worry (Josephus, *J.W.* 1.145–47). He told his soldiers to fire no arrows at the Jews on the Sabbath because that would only give them license to launch a defensive counterattack. This reluctance to fight or carry weapons on the Sabbath was so well-known that generally Jews were not conscripted into the Roman army during the New Testament period (Josephus *Ant.* 14.226).

Another problem involved travel. In Exodus 16:29 the Lord instructed the people "to stay where they are on the seventh day." However, some movement was necessary—perhaps to visit a friend or step outside—and so the rule was set (based on Josh. 3:4) that one could move "2,000 cubits" from one's place or "domicile." A cubit is about eighteen inches (the distance from the elbow to the tip of the middle finger, or one short step), so a permitted Sabbath day's journey was about a half mile (see Acts 1:12). However, defining a domicile (or residence from which this distance was counted) became an enormous theological debate. It could be the entire city where you lived. Here is how it worked.

In Jesus' day, there was an interesting workaround. If a person walked 2,000 cubits from his domicile and there deposited some food or personal object, this could be a *temporary* domicile, and thus another 2,000 cubits could be walked (giving a person 4,000 cubits distance). This led to rivalries of families placing objects in public places to extend their domiciles (Mishnah, *ʿErubin* 6:2). Others declared their domicile as the region around their neighborhood so that they could walk to friends' homes or synagogue without marking the distance.

Today Orthodox Jews still extend their "domiciles" by quietly marking their neighborhoods with *eruvim* (generally wires or markers on telephone poles or trees). *Eruv* (plural *eruvim*) means "mixing," and the markers permit Jews to mix public and private domains in order to increase their domicile and thus not be limited by the Sabbath laws. Why? Because they never leave "home" when they are within these boundary markers.

JESUS AND FIVE SABBATH STORIES

I imagine that Jesus found all of this Sabbath legislation tiresome. And he may well have agreed with the rabbi who thought of these rules as "mountains hanging by a thread." That rabbi went on to say that the rules "hover in the air with nothing to support them" (Mishnah, Ḥagigah 1:8). And yet I am also certain that Jesus respected the Sabbath and viewed it as a day set apart. Nevertheless Sabbath rules became a flashpoint for his own ministry because faithfulness to the mountain of rules was one way that Jesus' Jewish audiences thought they were being faithful to God.

These discussions about what was permitted and not permitted on the Sabbath were well-known to Jesus and his disciples. As a faithful and obedient Jew, Jesus lived with utmost respect for the Sabbath (Mark 1:21; 6:2; Luke 4:16). But in a number of cases, he disagreed with the authorities about the restrictions that were being applied to it. On one occasion he expressed open exasperation regarding Sabbath rules: "The Sabbath was made for man, not man for the Sabbath" (Mark 2:27). In some manner, the Sabbath had evolved into something it was never intended to be.

The Gospels record five stories where Jesus finds himself in some conflict with the Jewish leadership regarding the Sabbath. When we read them, we can't help but wonder if Jesus is using Sabbath rules—or breaking Sabbath rules—to provoke a discussion about what true faithfulness to God looks like.

Plucking Grain

In Mark 2:23–38 (also in Matt. 12:1–14 and Luke 6:1–5) Jesus was walking through a grain field with his disciples. They plucked grain in the field, rubbed them in their hands, and ate. This met an objection from nearby Pharisees (were they following them?): "Look, why are they doing what is unlawful on the Sabbath?" (Mark 2:24). They were indeed "reaping," and this "work" is listed in Mishnah, *Shabbat* 7 as illegal. Jesus then responded by reminding them that in the Scripture itself (1 Sam. 21:1 – 6) King David once apparently broke the law when he ate the holy bread of the temple when he was hungry — and this was a more severe offense!

This is when Jesus explained three things. (1) The Sabbath was made for our benefit — not the other way around (Mark 2:27). (2) The essence of Sabbath life is not rigid legalism but mercy and generosity (Matt. 12:7). (3) And Jesus himself is "Lord of the Sabbath" (Luke 6:5) because in him something "greater than the temple" is present (Matt. 12:6). These were stunning things to say, and I am certain the Pharisees took notes and prepared for more conflict with him. They no doubt wondered: *Does Jesus think he has the authority to reinterpret the Sabbath?*

Healing a Man with a Deformed Hand

Another story centers on a man with a deformed hand (Mark 3:1 – 6; also in Matt. 12:9 – 14 and Luke 6:6 – 11). Healing on the Sabbath was only acceptable if the life of a person (or animal) was in jeopardy. Jesus reminded them of this (Mark 3:4) but was pragmatic. If a sheep falls into a pit but isn't in danger of dying, should we not rescue it anyway (Matt. 12:11)? But here the Pharisees wanted to test him. If a man had a deformed hand — and his life was not in danger — would you rescue him on the Sabbath? It seems clear that Jesus' reputation for Sabbath flexibility was well-known, and here they were testing his loyalty to its rules.

Here we gain an insight into Jesus' frustration: he "looked around at them in anger and [was] deeply distressed at their stubborn hearts" (Mark 3:5). Jesus promptly healed the man, and the response to him was equally strong. According to Luke 6:11, "the Pharisees and the teachers of the law were furious." Matthew and Mark tell that this event (and many others like it no doubt) set in motion a political plot to destroy Jesus. Ironically the very people who wanted to protect the holiness of the Sabbath used this day to plot a murder (Mark 3:6).

A Paralyzed Woman and a Sick Man

Luke records two incidents that are almost parallel to each other. Each occurred on the Sabbath and each involved desperately ill people. First, one Sabbath as Jesus was teaching in a synagogue, a woman was there who had been crippled for eighteen years (Luke 13:10 – 17). She may have had a back injury or scoliosis or a crippling condition we cannot identify. But she could not stand up straight. Jesus stopped his teaching, healed her, and saw in it an opportunity to teach. The ruler of the synagogue objected immediately, but Jesus then used an analogy from Jewish law: "Doesn't each of you on the Sabbath untie your ox or donkey from the stall and lead it out to give it water? Then should not this woman, a daughter of Abraham, whom Satan has kept bound for eighteen long years, be set free on the Sabbath day from what bound her?" (Luke 13:15 – 16). It was a victory, and the crowd as well as the leaders in the synagogue grasped his logic.

On another Sabbath—by now Luke says that the leaders were watching Jesus carefully on Sabbaths—Jesus was dining in the home of a village leader (Luke 14:1 – 6). A man suffering from an "abnormal swelling of his body" suddenly appeared. The technical term for this is *edema* (*oedema* in the U.K.; in Greek it is *hydropikos* [*hydro* refers to water]). This is acute swelling of the body, which the ancients thought was the holding of water in the tissues. Often it is most evident in the extremities of a person, such as their hands and feet, can be very painful, and often is related to heart failure. Today physicians have identified many types of edema and are still discovering its sources.

In this story Jesus forced the same question he had used before. *May a person heal on the Sabbath?* For him it represented an important idea, namely, that Sabbath faithfulness is not located in a scrupulous obedience to rules but should be seen as a day God has given to us. And as a part of that day, it is good and acceptable to do good deeds.

A Crippled Man in Jerusalem

John's gospel records two Sabbath stories. One in John 9 tells about a blind man whom Jesus healed on the Sabbath

ANCIENT REMAINS OF THE
POOL OF BETHESDA

(John 9:14). However the central theme of this story does not turn on the Sabbath but focuses rather on Jesus' struggle with the Pharisees and the theme of darkness. We do learn here, however, that Jesus was well-known for Sabbath violations, and it led his opponents to conclude that anyone who could not keep the Sabbath could not be from God (9:16).

The longest Sabbath conflict story we possess is recorded in John 5:1–47. Jesus was north of the temple at a pool called Beth-Zatha (some Greek texts call it Bethesda, "house of flowing"). It was an ancient pool used for water collection; in Jesus' day it had become a place for ritual bathing. A reservoir adjacent (north) to the pool fed water into Beth-Zatha through a hidden causeway, and when the water was stirred, some needy people believed that angels were moving in the water and healing might happen.[9] The pool had been lost for centuries but was discovered in the mid-twentieth century and is located adjacent to St. Anne's Church in Jerusalem's Old City.

At the pool Jesus found a paralyzed man who had been a paraplegic for thirty-eight years and who was hoping to slip into the water at an opportune time. Jesus interrupted his waiting, healed him, and told him to pick up his pallet and walk (John 5:8–9). The problem, of course, is that it was the Sabbath and we know (Mishnah, *Shabbat* 7:2) that carrying something like this was forbidden. Jerusalem has always been a city of religious zealots, and so it was that day. A Sabbath enforcer abruptly chastised the man, telling him that what he was doing was forbidden (John 5:10).

As this story unwinds, eventually the healed man met Jesus and discovered the true identity of his healer. Nevertheless, this work had been done on the Sabbath and the violation remained. But it is the nature of Jesus' defense that is fascinating. Judaism also understood that God worked on the Sabbath. He also sustained the universe and made things like the rain to fall. Babies were born and people died—and God was sovereign over these things pertaining to life and death. (This was the basis of the logic for why working to *save life* on the Sabbath made sense.) Now Jesus made the same claim. "My Father is always at his work to this very day, and I too am working" (5:17). Because God worked on the Sabbath—and Jesus claimed a connection with God—therefore he had the right to work on the Sabbath as well.

John's summary of these events is striking. In 5:16 John tells us that this sort of Sabbath violation was the reason Jesus was so aggressively opposed, and when he made an argument that in some manner gave him a divine right to speak to Sabbath

CHRIST AT THE POOL OF BETHESDA BY BARTOLOME ESTEBAN MURILLO DEPICTS JESUS HEALING ON THE SABBATH.

rules, his behavior was absolutely unacceptable to the authorities (5:18). Because the Sabbath belonged exclusively to God, the Sabbath became a platform from which Jesus could unveil the deeper nature of his authority and his relationship with God. His Sabbath violations no doubt became characteristic of much of his ministry. They were minor violations, symbolic violations perhaps, where in doing good things (and promoting the life-giving interests of God) he was accused of spiritual presumption.

The wider question of the Gospels is this: Can the purposes of God for the Sabbath be buried in human legislation? The answer is most certainly "yes" — and then it is left to the "Lord of the Sabbath" (Luke 6:5) to come and set things right.

FAITH AND THE SABBATH

I mentioned in chapter 1 that some years ago when our children were young, we lived in an Orthodox Jewish neighborhood in Chicago. It was fun to learn about Jewish traditions, be invited to Sabbath dinners, and witness how they celebrated their festivals. But the Sabbath always posed some unique social challenges. For instance, we always moved our daughters' birthdays to Sunday afternoon so the neighbor girls could come over (thereby avoiding the Sabbath). We simply asked them to do the same for us.

One Saturday morning in spring I was in the front yard with my daughters using grass seed to patch bare spots on the lawn. They wanted to help. Soon they were scattering seed in most of the wrong places, but it was fun, so I let them. But at about that time our local synagogue was dismissing and two little girls came running down the sidewalk, asking if they could join in. Of course I invited them. But as soon as they started tossing the seed around, suddenly I heard the yells of their parents from a block away. "Stop immediately! It's Sabbath!" When they arrived and seemed quite angry, they explained that the law forbad sowing seed on the Sabbath — and I had helped their children break the Sabbath.

Of course I argued that they weren't *sowing* seed at all. In fact, I wish they had sowed a bit of seed because most of it was on the sidewalk. But there we were, doing precisely what the ancient rabbis wrote about: discussing the finer interpretations of the law.

"But they picked it up and threw it," the parents said.

"Yes" I countered, "but it isn't sowing unless it serves to plant something."

"I know, but the law is the law. No touching seed!"

"They were just having fun," I pleaded.

The final retort: "This is not Sabbath fun." And the family left for home.

That moment ended poorly, but it brought to my mind immediately the many pages I had read in the Mishnah and Jesus' public struggles with the custodians of Sabbath law. To me there is a difference between working on the Sabbath as a farmer, sowing seed that will germinate, and being a child tossing Scott's Bermuda grass seed into the wind.

Jesus was among those Jewish teachers who championed leniency and freedom over binding rules. He viewed the Sabbath as something designed to bless us as well as an opportunity to worship God. However, the society in which I live is not burdened by legalism on the Sabbath. It is instead so consumed by liberty that Sabbath (or for us, Sunday) has lost most of its meaning. When many of my friends think about Sunday, they think about shopping and football.

Christian author Marva Dawn reminds us of what we've lost. In her compelling book *Keeping the Sabbath Wholly*, Dawn traces the value of the Sabbath not simply in its biblical legacy, but she examines how necessary it is for us to build this God-given rhythm into our lives. This is not about obeying; this is about enjoying something good that God has planned for us.

Ironically if Jesus were here with us today, I wonder if he might open a conversation not about our Sabbath rules (what rules?!) but about our lack of intentionality for this day. He might ask us how we are weaving this rhythm of rest purposefully into our lives. How are we respecting the fourth commandment? It would be a prophetic word indeed. We might experience the same discomfort as those Jewish leaders did in the first century.

We are a people who cannot simply cease to do things. *We struggle with the notion of rest at a profound cultural level.* And because of this, we mismanage this weekly gift perhaps as sorely as anyone in the first century.

Chapter 3

JESUS AND THE PASSOVER

John 6:1–71

THE ANNUAL feast of Passover (Heb. *Pesach*) has been the
defining festival of Judaism for over three thousand years.
Not only does it mark the passage from winter to spring when
new life emerges (for both the farmer and the shepherd), but
it marks the restoration of Israel's national life that concluded
its four-hundred-year captivity in Egypt. It is a story of political and spiritual liberation centered on the most important
character of Israel's salvation story: Moses.

Within Jewish homes, both in the ancient world and today,
a sacrificial meal was shared (or today it is remembered), the
great story of salvation told, and hope is rekindled that this
Passover redemption will continue to follow Israel's ongoing history. In Jesus' day, these festivities were centered at
the Jerusalem temple, and, whenever possible, every pious
Jewish family would strive to make the trek to Jerusalem to
participate.

Modern Western Christianity has little like it. Sadly many
modern churches barely know how to anchor our "defining
story" into a festival calendar like Judaism. We once did, however. The great centering feast of the church has always been

Easter and the days immediately preceding it. "Holy Week" (the days from Palm Sunday to Easter) records for us the great events of *our story*. Jesus' final arrival in Jerusalem, his interrogation and sacrificial death, and his resurrection mark the defining events for our Christian understanding. According to ancient intricate liturgies (now preserved by many liturgical churches), believers have been keeping vigil the Saturday night before Easter for nearly two thousand years. Before Jerusalem became a Muslim city in the seventh century, the great Byzantine churches of Jerusalem had vast and elaborate celebrations that can be partially glimpsed today at the Church of the Holy Sepulcher. A visit to the great "Ceremony of Holy Fire" led by the Greek Orthodox Patriarch of Jerusalem the night before Easter (a ceremony now a thousand years old) will give you a hint of the scale of this sort of festival.

Ironically the Great Story of the church falls within the Great Story of Judaism. Both look for deeper meanings in Passover.

JUDAISM AND THE PASSOVER

The Old Testament background for this festival began in Egypt, and its telling provided an essential foundation to God's people who needed to comprehend their spiritual legacy. It

Todd Bolen/www.BiblePlaces.com

THE ISRAELITES WOULD SPREAD THE BLOOD OF A SACRIFICED LAMB ON THEIR DOORPOSTS AT PASSOVER.

HYSSOP WAS USED TO SPREAD THE BLOOD ON THE DOORPOSTS.

was a story that began with a protected life in Egypt following the life of Joseph (Gen. 47:1−6). But after four centuries, the Israelites had become slaves (Ex. 1:8−14). Passover is the story of their rescue: God raised up a prophet (Moses) who defeated Egypt's Pharaoh with ten devastating plagues (Ex. 7−12). Moses then led the tribes across the eastern deserts and on through a miraculously opened sea. During three months of desert travel they were fed with manna and quail—and miraculous supplies of water. Moses then brought them to God's holy mountain, Mount Sinai, where the Lord made a covenant with Israel (Ex. 19−20).

Passover gains its name from the final plague that required the life of every firstborn son in Egypt, from Pharaoh's son to cattle (Ex. 11). The Israelites, however, were spared because

UNLEAVENED BREAD

A Passover sacrifice

they marked their homes with the blood of a sacrificed lamb so that death would "bypass" (Heb. *pesach* translated as *passover*) their families (12:1–13). The lamb (or goat, 12:5) was sacrificed, and a brush made from a hyssop bush spread some blood on the vertical posts and the lintel of every Israelite home's door. And that night, as the firstborn males of Egypt died and Pharaoh relented, a meal was eaten that would forever commemorate Israel's redemption.

Through the prophet Moses, God explained: "The blood shall be a sign for you on the houses where you live: when I see the blood, I will pass over you, and no plague shall destroy you when I strike the land of Egypt" (Ex. 12:13 NRSV).

Three ceremonies eventually were woven into the festivities of Passover. The Passover sacrifice was anchored in the death of the lamb that was sacrificed in Egypt to save the Israelite families. But in addition, Israel celebrated a feast of "unleavened bread" (or yeast-free bread) each spring, and in the Passover ceremony in Egypt, unleavened bread was a meal requirement (Ex. 12:17–20). Finally, to set a reminder of what had happened in Egypt during the tenth plague, Israel was told to set apart the firstborn of all children and beasts as belonging to the Lord (Ex. 13:1–2). The children would be redeemed in a ceremony (13:13), but this enactment was built in order to remind all Israel of the costliness of their salvation and the wondrous power of God: "the LORD brought us out of Egypt with his mighty hand" (Ex. 13:16).

JESUS AND PASSOVER

Since Jesus was a faithful Jew, it is easy to imagine that he observed the Passover festival every year. Because of this we try to use references to Passover in the Gospels to calculate the length of Jesus' ministry. But here there is a problem. Matthew, Mark, and Luke only refer to one Passover, the one at the end of his ministry when he was crucified (Mark 14:1). Surely Jesus' ministry did not last only one year. John, however, provides more references (John 2:13; 6:4; 11:55), and it is on the basis of these that many conclude that Jesus' ministry lasted three years. The Gospel writers did not feel compelled to record every reference to Jesus' festival participation (there is only one reference to Tabernacles, John 7:2), and so it may be impossible to answer this issue definitively.

By the first century, Jewish festival traditions had evolved and expanded enormously—as they would in any tradition. Passover was a pilgrimage festival that called on all Jews to travel to Jerusalem for a week in celebration. Did everyone attend? This is unlikely since it would have left countless villages all over the country abandoned. But many did come, both from within the country and from distant lands. We estimate that the population of Jerusalem swelled from about 30,000 to perhaps 75,000 or 100,000 during the Passover feast.[10]

Jewish days began at sunset, and so the Passover began at sunset on the fifteenth day of the Jewish springtime month of Nisan. (The Jewish calendar is lunar and so Passover officially is marked from the first new moon following the spring equinox.) Two days before (Nisan 13 generally) Jewish homes removed all traces of yeast from their houses. This included everything from bread to beer (Mishnah, *Pesachim* 3:1). Even crumbs had to be hunted down in the corners of the cellar. On Nisan 14 (the afternoon before sunset) the lambs (or goats) were slaughtered. And, following Leviticus 23, the festival was kept for eight days (Nisan 15–22).

A man and perhaps his sons would carry their Passover ani-

THE JEWISH HOLIDAYS FOLLOW
A LUNAR CALENDAR.

mal to the temple, and there a priestly assistant (a Levite) would inspect it and manage its slaughtering. Blood from the lamb was caught in a silver or gold bowl, passed to other Levites, and then was cast at the base of the sacrificial altar (Mishnah, *Pesachim* 5:5–7). All the while, the Levites were chanting Psalms 113–118, the Hallel (or "praise") Psalms. The carcass was then hung on meat hooks on the temple walls and pillars, and its kidneys and liver removed and burned (Lev. 3:3–4); then the body was returned to the waiting family for roasting. Even here the law specifies how it should be roasted—on a wooden skewer (not a metal one or a grill)—and it was often basted with fruit juice.

Families in large groups camped around the walled city. Care was taken to avoid the

THE EIGHTEENTH-CENTURY *BOOK OF CUSTOMS* SHOWS JEWS CLEANING AND GETTING RID OF ALL LEAVENED BREAD FOR PASSOVER.

many cemeteries surrounding Jerusalem (which were clearly marked). Contact with these would make a family unclean and so unable to celebrate the feast. Then on the night of Passover, they fulfilled the law by eating the Passover meal inside the city itself. Families would join together until there were enough people to consume the roasted young lamb or goat that had been sacrificed that afternoon. This was the ideal scenario. But scholars suspect that this meal was also celebrated throughout the country and not just in Jerusalem.

We know little about the formalities of the meal. Today's Passover "Seder" (which means *ordering*) was organized in the late first century after the destruction of the temple in AD 70. Today, after two thousand years, it has taken on numerous innovations. But in Jesus' day, we believe it was organized around four cups of (red) wine, the singing of the Hallel Psalms (Psalms 113 – 118), and the eating of bitter herbs, unleavened bread (yeast-free bread), and a dish called *haroset* (a mixture of apples, nuts, and wine).[11] In the first century, the telling of the Passover story (Heb. *haggadah*) became common so that the meal was also an instructional evening particularly for children. After the fourth cup of wine, the gathering dispersed into the night.

The symbols of the meal pointed to the meaning of the Passover story. After the second cup of wine, a son might ask,

THE MOUNT OF OLIVES IS FILLED WITH SOME OF THE MANY CEMETERIES SURROUNDING JERUSALEM.

© Vlad and Ludmila Chernovs/www.istockphoto.com

THE TRADITIONAL ELEMENTS OF
A PASSOVER SEDER MEAL

"Why is this night different than other nights?" (Mishnah, *Pesachim* 10:4). And the food itself would speak the story: the bitter herbs reminded them of their tears in Egypt, the *haroset* recalled the mortar of slave-built bricks, and unleavened bread pointed to the hasty meal cooked the night of their escape. Rabbi Gamaliel (who lived in Jesus' era) said plainly that failure to recite the meaning of this meal was a failure to keep it at all.

Baker Photo Archive, courtesy of the Masada Museum

FIRST-CENTURY CUPS THAT COULD HAVE
BEEN USED FOR PASSOVER WINE

A Passover Miracle

The celebrated hero of Passover is Moses, and within the Passover story his great efforts to liberate Israel stand out. Moses had defeated Pharaoh. Moses led Israel through the sea. Moses guided them through the desert for three months until they came to Mount Sinai, where a covenant with God was ratified. Among the rabbis one of the most remarkable miracles produced by Moses was the miracle of manna, when each morning the Israelites were fed with a wafer-like bread. Manna means in Hebrew "What is it?"—and this is what they thought when they saw it on the first morning. The

HAROSET, A MIXTURE OF APPLES, NUTS, AND WINE

Jonathan David Thoreson

ARTWORK OF THE MANNA MIRACLE FROM A DOMINICAN ORDER CHURCH IN FRIESACH, AUSTRIA

Wikimedia Commons

manna began when Israel left Egypt, and it continued until they entered the Promised Land (Ex. 16:35).

How did this manna happen? In Jewish lore in that period, many believed that Moses' righteousness opened a "treasury" of manna each morning. The treasury opened, manna spilled out on the people, and then the treasury closed and withdrew. When the Israelites crossed the Jordan River, the treasury closed permanently. Judaism's fervent hope was that in some future time, God would send a hero forged on the model of Moses (Deut. 18:15), who would duplicate the miracle of Moses: he would be able to revive the treasury once again, he would return the prowess of Moses, and he would bring about a liberation that (in Jesus' day) Jews yearned for. They looked for "bread from heaven" just as Moses had given it (Ps. 78:25). An ancient Jewish writing called 2 *Baruch* puts it clearly: "The treasury of manna shall again descend from on high, and they will eat of it in those years" (2 *Bar.* 29:8). An ancient Jewish commentator on the book of Ecclesiastes wrote, "As the first redeemer caused manna to descend . . . so will the latter redeemer cause manna to descend" (Midrash Rabbah, *Ecclesiastes* 1.9).

It is no accident that Jesus fed the five thousand during Passover season (John 6:4). But what we find is that Passover themes were swirling around almost every aspect of the story.

The story opens with Jesus on a Galilee hillside with an extremely large gathering of Jews. They were hungry. "Where shall we buy bread for these people to eat?" (John 6:5) is the question Jesus asked his disciples, but this question could have been asked among the Israelites three days after they left Egypt during the first Passover. Notice how Mark describes the people: they are seated in groups by hundreds and fifties—all on green grass (Mark 6:39–40). Any shepherd would imme-

JESUS OFTEN GATHERED ON THE GALILEE
HILLSIDES WITH HIS FOLLOWERS.

JESUS AND THE JEWISH FESTIVALS

diately recognize the image. *Jesus is a shepherd feeding his flock.* As Moses the shepherd (Ex. 3:1) led Israel out of Egypt and fed them in the wilderness, now Jesus the shepherd does the same.

When Jesus provided miraculous bread (John 6:11), immediately the crowds in Galilee drew out the next conclusion. "Surely this is the Prophet who is to come into the world" (6:14). Here we have a direct echo of Deuteronomy 18:15 and 18, promising the coming of a prophet like Moses. The crowd saw it clearly: Jesus was duplicating the feeding miracle of Passover just like Moses. Was Jesus the new Moses?

At once, Jesus took his disciples and put them on a boat to cross the Sea of Galilee while he departed for the mountains in the north. The crowd's enthusiastic deduction about Moses had led them to an unfortunate next step. *They tried to take Jesus and force him to be their king!* (John 6:15). So he departed hastily. The disciples remained at sea on the boat till it was dark, when a storm arose. But then they saw Jesus—walking on the sea to meet them. "It is I; don't be afraid" (6:20).[12]

Again, here we have another theme from Passover—a water miracle—that reminds us of the moment when Moses led Israel through the sea (Ex. 13–15). Psalm 77 describes this moment in Israel's life and explains that it was in fact God who led them.

Hills above Galilee near Mount Meron

The waters saw you, God,
> *the waters saw you and writhed;*
> *the very depths were convulsed. . . .*
Your path led through the sea,
> *your way through the mighty waters,*
> *though your footprints were not seen.*
You led your people like a flock
> *by the hand of Moses and Aaron. (Ps. 77:16, 19 – 20)*

Moses was a shepherd leading his people through the sea! Now Jesus was doing the same.

When the boat arrived at the fishing village of Capernaum, the people who had seen the miracle pressed him further for answers. Their entire conversation in the synagogue turned on one essential question: "What sign then will you give that we may see it and believe you? What will you do? Our ancestors ate the manna in the wilderness; as it is written: 'He gave them bread from heaven to eat'" (John 6:30 – 31). We might put this another way: *Have you repeated the great sign of Moses? Like Moses, have you given us "bread from heaven" to eat?* Once again the theme is Passover. The bread miracle has been repeated. The treasury of heaven has been opened. If Jesus is the custodian of the heavenly treasury, surely he has some connection with Moses.

THE SEA OF GALILEE

© William D. Mounce

THE CAPERNAUM SYNAGOGUE

But the audience in the synagogue at Capernaum offered a challenge. If it is true that in the days of Moses the treasury of manna was opened, and if it is true that Jesus was making some messianic claim, then what sort of sign could Jesus give to validate his word? Could he reopen the treasury (John 6:30–31)? Was he claiming that he had recreated the messianic Moses miracle?

Jesus' interpretation of the manna follows rabbinic lines perfectly. First, the true source of the manna was not Moses but God. It was God who sent bread. Furthermore, the manna story went beyond mere bread—it was a spiritual metaphor for how God feeds us with his word. Deuteronomy 8:3 might well have entered Jesus' debate, "[God] humbled you, causing you to hunger and then feeding you with manna, which neither you nor your ancestors had known, to teach you that man does not live on bread alone but on every word that comes from the mouth of the Lord."

If it is true that God is the source of true heavenly bread—and if it is true that Jesus has been sent by God—the shocking turn in John 6:33 should come as no surprise. The bread of God is a person (he who "comes down from heaven"), a person who gives life to the world. With a stroke of genius, Jesus has done precisely what he was planning with the miracle: he has exploited the central feature of Passover and applied it to himself. He is the manna from God's treasury for which Israel has been waiting. He had been sent by God as manna descended in the wilderness.

Jesus now presses the logic of his case to the next level: "I am the bread" of Passover, the heavenly manna, the contents of God's divine treasury: "I am the bread of life" (John 6:35). He supplies what Judaism sought in its Passover activities and stories. As the people were yearning for the heavenly bread—and as the rabbis reinterpreted this bread to mean the life-sustaining presence of God—now Jesus is that precious gift (cf. 6:48, 51).

This was a scandalous development. Jesus was not merely comparing himself to Passover, but supplying in himself the "promise" of Passover. This was the great turning point that the synagogue audience could not bear. It was one thing to say that we should have faith in God and be fed by him, but it was quite another for Jesus to say that he was the source of that meal, the object of belief. The "grumbling" described in John 6:41, 43 (and 51) is another Passover echo. It reminds us of the "murmuring" of the Israelites in the desert when they turned against Moses in the wilderness.

FAITH AND PASSOVER

If Sabbath reminds us of the renewing routines of rest, Passover recalls the importance of remembering. Israel's principal responsibility was not simply to serve up a meal with elaborate traditional recipes. Israel's responsibility was to understand the meal, why it was established, and what Great Story stood behind it. The telling of the exodus-to-Sinai story was so central to the meal that surely without it, the meal was reduced to sentimentality. Israel followed a God who stepped into history, saved his people, and brought them to himself. Remembering this alone through recitation and a liturgical meal anchored Israel annually in the Great Story of its salvation.

We are the same. The Great Story of our faith is also a story recited. It begins on Palm Sunday and continues to Easter, recounting the great deeds of God worked out in Jesus' death and resurrection. Our Great Story is set in Passover too (see chapter 6). It is our anchoring story in which God shows his single-handed act of salvation to bring us to himself. To live through Holy Week, to celebrate the Lord's Supper (or Eucharist), to dress up at Easter and not be able to tell our story is like a Jew celebrating the *Pesach* and not knowing the great struggle between Moses and Pharaoh. To not know the meaning of Good Friday would be equivalent to a Jew not understanding that a lamb's blood saved Israel's firstborn. It is sad beyond measure.

THE CROSS IS THE CENTRAL SYMBOL AT EASTER. OUR EASTER STORY IS ENTWINED WITH THE HISTORY OF THE JEWISH PASSOVER.

But faith is more than recitation. It also has a present dimension. Faith is not merely remembering; it is believing and trusting. On the Passover of John 6, Jesus not only fed five thousand people and reminded them of their Great Story, but he explicitly fulfilled it. And when they wondered if he was the new Moses who could control the manna treasury, he corrected them and said that he *was* the manna itself ("I am the bread of life," John 6:35) who had "come down from heaven" (6:38). Moreover, eating this bread (consuming Jesus!) would be made possible by his death on the cross (6:51). Jesus concluded: "This is the bread that came down from heaven. Your ancestors ate manna and died, but whoever feeds on this bread will live forever" (6:58). Therefore celebrating Passover is not only knowing about what happened yesterday—though this is important—it is also about knowing the God who desires to feed us now.

A living Passover, then, required the consumption of living bread—not merely the bread of remembering. These are the twin themes of our story. A vital faith knows its Great Story (it can recite the past), and it has a personal encounter with God (in the present). To fail in either assignment is to be left like the crowd remaining in Capernaum's synagogue—confused, questioning, and murmuring. But to understand it—how reciting the past and believing the present work together—is to become like Peter, who stood in the Capernaum synagogue and announced his commitment to everything Jesus had taught (John 6:66–69).

Chapter 4

JESUS AND TABERNACLES

John 7–9

FEW OF us are aware of the agricultural cycles of nature. South America and southern Europe ship us strawberries in winter and we rarely think about it. Israel ships us flowers in January and few notice. My local grocery store's fruit/vegetable section barely changes from month to month.

It was only sixty years ago that this was not the case. Our food came in seasons. And a hundred years ago when many more Americans lived on farms, the cycle of food growth, harvest, and storage was a part of life. Our one remnant of this cycle is Thanksgiving. It should be a festival marking the end of the harvest and filling us with thanks for the bounty. Now it is a celebration of family and generic "thanks" for what has gone well for us. The Pilgrims no doubt saw it differently. Winter was coming, they had safe food stores after harvest, and it was time to thank God.

Israel was keenly aware of its own food cycles. This was an agrarian society that recognized the threat of a failed harvest and the gift of surplus food. As we have seen (chapter 1) the festivals of Judaism followed this cycle. The springtime Passover (or *Pesach*) festival welcomed newly born animals and the incoming cereal

A PRIESTLY BLESSING BEING GIVEN AT THE WESTERN WALL

THE SEVEN BLESSED SPECIES OF THE PROMISED LAND: GRAPES, FIGS, OLIVES, POMEGRANATES, DATES, BARLEY, AND WHEAT

harvest. Now the cereal harvest could begin in earnest. The barley fields were cut first, and then followed the harvest of wheat.

Seven weeks later, before the onset of summer's heat, a second festival called Pentecost (or *Shavuot*) commemorated the end of the grain harvest. This was the first day when farmers could bring their "firstfruits" (Heb. *bikkurim*) to the temple (Mishnah, *Bikkurim* 1:3). The law required that they bring only items from among the seven "species" of Deuteronomy 8:8. A farmer would watch his fields, and the first grain to ripen was tied off with reed grass. These were then harvested separately, collected in baskets, and taken to Jerusalem for the festival of Pentecost in a joyous procession (Deut. 26; Mishnah, *Bikkurim* 3:1–12). Two loaves of bread were then offered as a sacrifice.

Central to these celebrations was barley. Barley (which the Romans called *farina*) is one of humanity's most important crops. It was domesticated quite early (about 8000 BC), and some have argued that its cultivation in the Middle East and Europe led to the prospering of those civilizations.[13] When Moses described the bounty of the Promised Land in Deuteronomy 8:8, barley was listed as one of seven species found there. This grain was

MODEL OF BEER MAKING IN ANCIENT EGYPT,
LOCATED AT THE ROSICRUCIAN EGYPTIAN
MUSEUM IN SAN JOSE, CALIFORNIA

widely used for bread making. But also it was used for beer, a well-known beverage throughout Israel.[14] In the NIV Bible the phrase "fermented drink" generally refers to the Hebrew *shek-har*—a word that occurs about twenty times in the Old Testament. We now believe that this word refers to barley "beer" (as the NIV sometimes translates the word; see Prov. 31:6–7). Barley bread was soaked in water for days until it produced a sweet syrup. Then yeast was added until it bubbled (from alcohol and carbon dioxide). It was then filtered and drunk immediately.

JUDAISM AND TABERNACLES

Summer in Israel was a time to thresh, winnow, and mill the cereal harvest. But by late summer, everyone was awaiting the ripening of vine and tree. By October, the harvest season came to an end when grapes, olives, pomegranates, figs, and dates were gathered in. This launched the third great festival of the year called Tabernacles (Heb. *Sukkoth*). The feast was officially scheduled for the fifteenth day of the Jewish month of Tishri (five days after the Day of Atonement), and it lasted for seven days. One more festival day was added (Lev. 23:33–36), making the feast eight days long. This final festival day was called "the great day" of Sukkoth.

CHAPTER FOUR, JESUS AND THE TABERNACLES   69

Todd Bolen/www.BiblePlaces.com

WOMAN HARVESTING OLIVES

According to the law, all Israel was to live in "booths" or *sukkoth* (singular: *sukkah*; Lev. 23:42) during the celebration. These were outdoor shelters made from wild branches of olive, myrtle, palm, and other leafy trees (Neh. 8:15). They were built in Jerusalem during the pilgrimage feast. Residents likely built them on their roofs; pilgrim-travelers built them free standing outside Jerusalem's walls.

Todd Bolen/www.BiblePlaces.com

PUTTING PALMS ON THE ROOF OF A *SUKKAH*

FIELD SHELTERS ARE MADE OF STONE TO WATCH OVER AND PROTECT THE CROPS.

A *sukkah* was a temporary dwelling. ("Tabernacle" is an old English word made popular in the KJV [358 times] for the sanctuary-tent Israel built in the wilderness after they left Egypt.) Sometimes they are called booths (e.g., "the Festival of Booths"), but it all points to the same thing. During the fall harvest, because of the high value of the crops and the ease of stealing them, farmers would commonly build shelters in their fields to protect their crops. These "field shelters" are now made of stone and can be seen today throughout the Middle East, particularly in Palestine.

THE PALM, MYRTLE, AND WILLOW BRANCHES IN A *LULAV* COMBINE WITH AN *ETROG* TO MAKE UP THE "FOUR SPECIES."

Since this was the formal end of the harvest year, it was a time of celebration and revelry. Families brought samples of their harvest to Jerusalem and praised God for the completion of the year's bounty. Each person gathered up branches from palm, myrtle, and willow trees and wrapped their stems together to make a "waving palm" called a *lulav*. This was joined together with a citrus fruit called an *etrog*, and all four (called "the four species") were waved during temple ceremonies.

The people joined parades of pilgrims at the temple, and as they marched holding the *lulav*, they sang the Hallel Psalms (Psalms 113–118). When they came to 118:1 ("Give thanks to the LORD, for he is good") and 118:25 ("LORD, save us!"), the crowd was permitted to wave their "four species" in the air (Mishnah, *Sukkah* 3:9). This was the largest and most popular festival of the year. And surprising things could happen. One year, a self-appointed (and dubious) prophet named Joshua son of Ananias stirred things up. During one festival he stood up at the temple and yelled that God was condemning Jerusalem and the temple to judgment. The crowd couldn't stand it and he was pelted a hundred etrogs![15]

One example of how this tradition of waving palms appears in the New Testament is in the Gospels. When Jesus entered Jerusalem during his last Passover, the crowds instinctively picked up palms and waved them in celebration (John 12:13). Today when children wave palm fronds in church on Palm Sunday, they are actually using a remnant of the Jewish *lulav* tradition. The Hebrew word *lulav* literally refers to an *unfolded palm leaf*.

In Jesus' era this tradition continued and was enriched. Ceremonies around the temple were extensive and celebrations were full. Here is a description of Sukkoth from the Mishnah that may well offer an idealized picture of the celebration.

> *Men of piety and good works used to dance before them with burning torches in their hands singing songs and praises. And countless Levites [played] on harps, lyres, cymbals, and trumpets and instruments of music on the fifteen steps leading down from the Court of the Israelites to the Court of the Women, corresponding to the fifteen Songs of Ascents in the Psalms [Pss. 120–134]; upon them [the steps] the Levites used to stand with instruments of music and make melody. (Mishnah, Sukkah 5:4)[16]*

Sacrifice was another form of praise to God. And the sacrifices in the temple were astounding. On the first day the

FOURTH-CENTURY *LULAV* MOSAIC
AT THE TIBERIAS SYNAGOGUE

priests killed thirteen oxen, fourteen lambs, two rams, and a male goat. These were sacrifices for the sin of the people but also sacrifices of worship. Each day the number of oxen was reduced by one till the feast was over.

But agriculture was not the only interest at Sukkoth—or any of the other festivals. In each case, the pilgrimage festivals call up some aspect of Israel's "Great Story" of redemption. The story tells of Israel fleeing Egypt (Passover), coming to Mount Sinai to receive the covenant (Pentecost), and finally forty years (two at Mount Sinai, thirty-eight wandering in the desert) in the wilderness (Tabernacles). When they lived in the desert, they worshiped God at his "Sukkah" (tent, tabernacle) and built shelters for themselves as well. The Feast of Sukkoth, then, was also a time to retell the story of desert life and the temptations and victories found there. Leviticus made the connection explicit:

> *Live in temporary shelters for seven days: All native-born Israelites are to live in such shelters so your descendants will know that I had the Israelites live in temporary shelters when I brought them out of Egypt. I am the LORD your God. (Lev. 23:42–43)*

WATER AND LIGHT AT TABERNACLES

We can see here a variety of threads woven together in Tabernacles. There were agricultural celebrations rejoicing in the harvest, and there were historical teachings about the desert and Israel's wanderings. I can easily imagine Jesus as a young man traveling to Jerusalem every autumn with countless families from Galilee making a long caravan. And there in Jerusalem he joined in the revelry, waving his *lulav*, dancing and singing in the courtyards of the temple, perhaps trying his hand with an instrument. He slept on a hill under a leafy shelter with his parents outside the city, and they retold stories together from the books of Exodus and Numbers. He had the Hallel Psalms memorized and could sing them with ease. To have a fully Jewish life, Jesus certainly had fully Jewish festival experiences such as these.

The Water Ceremony

We also know that in this period two other ceremonies evolved, and Jesus knew these too. In October, Judaism recognized two concerns of the season. First, late autumn is a period of drought in Israel. Strong, drenching rains had not been seen since spring. Cisterns were low. Springs were becoming weak.

CISTERN AT MASADA. CISTERNS CAN BECOME LOW OR COMPLETELY DRY DURING A DROUGHT.

The hills were parched. The ground could not be renewed without water. Therefore Tabernacles incorporated a set of symbols depicting a prayer for water that would replenish the country agriculturally as well as refresh the land spiritually. In fact, rainfall during Tabernacles was a sign of strong blessing from God for the coming season. Even today Arabs surrounding modern Israel watch the country to see if it rains during Tabernacles. If it rains, it's a good omen for the rainy season to come.

CRACKING MUD IN THE WILDERNESS OF PARAN
SHOWS THE DEVASTATING EFFECTS OF DROUGHT.

Each day of the Feast of Tabernacles witnessed a water cer-emony in which a procession of priests descended to the south border of the city to the Gihon Spring (which flowed into the Pool of Siloam). There a priest filled a golden pitcher as a choir chanted Isaiah 12:3, "With joy you will draw water from the wells of salvation." The water was then carried back up the hill to the "Water Gate," followed by crowds carrying a *lulav* in the right hand and an *etrog* in the left. The crowd would shake these and sing the Hallel Psalms before the priests.

When the procession arrived at the temple, the priest climbed the altar steps and poured the water onto the altar while the crowd circled him and continued singing. Two silver bowls rested on top of the altar; each had a spout with a small hole. The priest poured water into one bowl; then he poured wine into the other, and both drained simultaneously onto the altar (Mishnah, *Sukkah* 4:9). According to later Jewish tradi-tion (AD 400), this pouring was intended to remind everyone of the water that came from the rock in the wilderness (Ex. 17:1–7; Num. 20:8–13)—another story repeated at Taberna-cles.[17] On the great and final day of the festival, this water pro-cession took place seven times, drenching the altar thoroughly.

Judaism saw this water ceremony on multiple levels. On the one hand, it was a plea to God for rain. But on the other hand, it

THE WATER CEREMONY

was a source of rich symbolism. In the wilderness, God brought water from rock (Num. 20:8, 10), and here water was flowing from the sacrificial rock altar of the temple. Ezekiel and Zechariah had visions of rivers flowing from the temple in a miraculous display of God's blessing (Ezek. 47:1; Zech. 14:8). In a drought-stricken land, it was a spectacular vision of water—life-giving water flowing from God's life-giving temple.

The Light Ceremony

Second, people in the ancient world observed the length of days carefully, charting the solstices as well as the fall and spring equinox. Tabernacles coincided with the autumn equinox, when day and night are equal length—and from this point on in the calendar, the nights lengthen and the days become shorter. Jewish ritual practice recognized this "dying of the sun" and incorporated into the feast ceremonies of light to hallmark the passing of the season.

The Mishnah tractate *Sukkah* provides lavish descriptions of the light ceremonies and explains that whoever has not seen these things has never seen a wonder in his or her life! Four large stands each held four golden bowls, which were placed in the heavily used

The Jewish Temple

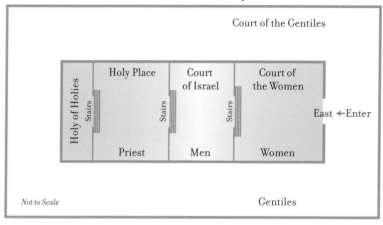

Court of the Women. These sixteen golden bowls (reached by ladders) were filled with oil, and for wicks they floated in them the knotted, worn undergarments of the priests (Mishnah, *Sukkah* 5:3). When they were lit at night (the rabbis said) all Jerusalem was illumined. In a world that did not have public lighting after dusk, this light shining from Jerusalem's yellow limestone walls must have been spectacular. Choirs of Levites sang during the lighting while "men of piety and good works" danced in the Court of the Women, carrying torches and singing hymns.

LADDERS CLIMBED THE LARGE STANDS
EACH HOLDING FOUR GOLDEN BOWLS

The evening closed with a dramatic procession. Levites stood on the fifteen steps above the Women's Court. They blasted trumpets on each step as they stepped down, walking east through the Women's Court. But when they reached the eastern gate, they turned around and faced west (toward the temple's Holy Place) and recited, "Our Fathers when they were in this place turned with their backs toward the Temple of the Lord and their faces toward the east, and they worshipped the sun toward the east; but as for us, our eyes are turned toward the Lord" (Mishnah, *Sukkah* 5:4). This liturgy was an explicit rejection of pagan life (worshiping the sun) and a full acknowledgment of faith in God (see Ezek. 8:16–17 for the same idea).

JESUS AND TABERNACLES

We possess only one record of Jesus visiting Jerusalem at Tabernacles (John 7–9). He was living in Galilee (no doubt Capernaum), and his family was on its way to the feast. His brothers did not believe in him (7:5) and were urging him (cynically perhaps?) to display his powers in Jerusalem during the feast. Jesus declined. And instead, he traveled there alone that year.

This was also a dangerous period for him. On his previous visit to Jerusalem, the leaders there threatened his life after he healed a paraplegic man on the Sabbath (John 5:18). Now the coming festival made those same leaders look for him when they saw the other members of Jesus' family (7:11). Public opinion about him was sharply divided—some thought he was sincere, others thought he was fraudulent. But because the authorities had formed severe opinions about him, most people stayed out of the coming fray (7:12–13). The word was out: if the authorities got a chance, they would kill him (7:25).

Sometime during the middle of the Feast of Tabernacles, as Jesus was teaching in the temple, he was interrogated by those same threatening authorities. John's account of this is abbreviated, and I imagine that the debates recorded in his gospel took many hours to unfold. But John summarizes them nicely. The leaders pursued three lines of argument.

First, how could Jesus teach with authority when he did not have the appropriate schooling? This was a problem. Jesus no doubt had the usual schooling natural to all young men, but formal schooling was over by the time he was twelve or thirteen. Advanced schooling was available in the oral law—and many young men moved to Jerusalem to study under the great rabbis of the day (Hillel, Gamaliel, or Johanan ben Zakkai perhaps). The apostle Paul did this (see Gal. 1:14; cf. Acts 22:3), but Jesus did not. Nevertheless for the next twenty years he attended regular synagogue gatherings, debating finer matters of the Scriptures. Yet Jesus made a remarkable claim during the feast in John 7. *His teaching was not from a human teacher, but from God himself* (John 7:16). This aligned him with the prophets, inspired directly by God, and yet he was capable of debating the minutia of the law with exacting precision (7:14–21).

Second, the authorities wanted to know where he came from. Jesus was known as "the prophet from Nazareth" in Galilee (Matt. 21:11), and for some, Galilee was an unlikely origin for the Messiah (John 7:41). He should come from the south, from Judea where Bethlehem is located (7:42). Some were dubious about anything that came from Nazareth (1:46), and later when the apostles were interrogated in Jerusalem, their Galilean heritage made the authorities fail to take them seriously. Still others held to the superstition that this Messiah would simply "appear" in Judea mysteriously (7:27). Jesus rejected all of these. His origins were important, but they were not what anyone expected: *Jesus' origins were in God himself* (7:29).

Third, Jesus was clear that he would eventually depart Jerusalem and Judea permanently and that where he was going, none of them would be able to follow. This led them to pursue a final question: Where did he plan to go where they could not follow? Did he plan to live among the Greeks (who were unclean)? And here Jesus' answer was the same as what we heard before: *Jesus was returning to God himself* (John 7:33).

Throughout the Feast of Tabernacles the incomprehension of the Jewish leaders stands out. Jesus' origin/teachings/destiny stemmed from heaven, and those looking for earthbound answers would always remain frustrated.

But it was on the last day, the "greatest day of the festival," that Jesus made a stir. Recall that this was the day of the great water festival when the altar was soaked seven times. And on this day Jesus stood among the people and called out: "Let anyone who is thirsty come to me and drink." This was a drought season! A good rain had not fallen in months! Tabernacles was sending prayers heavenward for rain every day! But what Jesus said next has to be read carefully. Some translations say:

"If anyone thirsts, let him come to me and drink. Whoever believes in me, as the Scriptures have said, 'Out of his [the believer's] heart shall flow rivers of living water.'"

We must decide who the pronoun "his" refers to. The Greek is ambiguous. Here the source of living water is found within the believer. But there is an entirely different and plausible way to translate this Greek sentence that a long list of scholars support:

"If anyone thirsts, let him come to me and let him who believes in me drink. As the scriptures have said, 'Out of his [Jesus'] heart shall flow rivers of living water.'"

Here Jesus is the *source* of the water yearned for at Tabernacles. Israel was to find in him what they were seeking in the festival. Jesus had taken one of the chief symbols of the festival and used it to explain his identity and work. The people heard this and immediately resistance melted away (John 7:40–41).

Then on that same day—or was it night? Were the light ceremonies in the Women's Court now underway? Did he interrupt the dancing and singing?—Jesus stood up again in the crowd and announced, "I am the light of the world. Whoever follows me will never walk in darkness, but will have the light of life" (John 8:12). If Joshua son of Ananias had been pelted with *etrogs* for interrupting the Feasts of Tabernacles one year, I wonder what sort of stir Jesus made. Imagine him standing beneath four of the golden bowls, their huge burning wicks lit, young men dancing, and Levitical trumpets poised to blast their descent to the eastern gate. Here in the great light ceremony of the year, Jesus makes the astounding claim to be the light of the world. The shock and irony must have been simply remarkable.

The rabbis in Jesus' day sought more than light and water in these ceremonies. Zechariah 14 was read during the feast, and there the prophet declared dramatically that God's light would come and banish darkness forever (Zech. 14:6) and that living water would flow continuously from the mountain of Jerusalem (14:8).

But more was needed in Israel's life. *Israel needed refreshment not merely through living water, but from God's own Spirit.* This is a standard Jewish interpretation well attested in our sources. The rabbis did not merely see the ceremonies as a literal plea for rain, but they saw this as a plea for ultimate blessing. The water of Zechariah 14 was viewed as a promise of the Holy Spirit. This is why John tells us that on the great Tabernacles Feast day Jesus was referring to the Holy Spirit in what he said. "By this he meant the Spirit, whom those who believed in him were later to receive" (John 7:39).

FAITH AND TABERNACLES

The Jewish Feast of Tabernacles is a helpful reminder that thanksgiving needs to be a vital part of our daily lives. In a wonderful essay on the centrality of gratitude for spiritual growth, Stan Guthrie notes how much research now proves that gratitude promotes emotional well-being, our sense of connection with the world, and a transformation in social attitudes.[18] While this is encouraging, Tabernacles does not look at thankfulness with a view to our benefit. Tabernacles promotes gratitude because it reminds us of our ultimate dependence on God and his provisions. It is what the faithful man or woman ought to do. I am reminded of the story of the ten lepers in Luke

GOD WAS GIVEN THANKS FOR THE BARLEY
AND OTHER CROP HARVESTS.

17 who were cured by Jesus. Only one turned back to express thanks. It is a story as well as a parable about human life.

At Tabernacles Israel looked back over the sweep of the year and was able to speak not merely a generic word of thanks, but gave specific thanks for the success of a completed agricultural season. From barley to sheep to pomegranates, God was given credit for sending goodness to his people. Of course there was labor (but labor without rain was futile). Of course there were human resources, human ingenuity, and time well spent. But a thoughtful person knows that the capacities and opportunities we enjoy often should be credited less to ourselves and more to others and to God. Tabernacles says: bring samples of what God has given you to the temple. And with them in hand, wrapped in your personal *lulav*, thank him.

Chapter 5

JESUS AND HANUKKAH

John 10

ANCIENT JUDAISM celebrated a number of minor festivals that are barely known to us today. Some of them have complicated origins. The three great pilgrimage festivals (Passover, Pentecost, and Tabernacles) enjoyed a long and rich biblical legacy, were celebrated by thousands, and even today continue to have a vibrant life in modern Judaism. But every culture has minor festivals as well. I think, for instance, about the American Presidents' Day. Originally it was designed in 1880 to celebrate our first president's birthday (George Washington, Feb. 22), but it was only recognized in Washington's federal offices. Then by 1885 all federal offices took the day off. But in the 1980s legislators desired to make a "Presidents' Day" that would also recognize Abraham Lincoln's birthday (Feb. 12), which was ten days from Washington's.

Now we have a bit of confusion. In most states Presidents' Day is a generic day to recognize America's presidents. But in Virginia (Washington's home state) it is "George Washington Day." Alabama inexplicably calls it "Washington and Jefferson Day" (to pull in Thomas Jefferson, who was born in April). For

Sebastian Scheiner/AP Images

JEWS PRAYING ON TISHA B'AV

most Americans, it is a day off from school and an afternoon to check sales at car dealerships.

First-century Judaism was likewise creative with its own minor festivals, and many of them evolved. Some were created after the biblical period. A few hundred years after Jesus Jews recognized what they called "Tisha B'Av," which translated to

Baker Photo Archive. Sola Scriptura.

SCROLL OF THE BOOK OF ESTHER

"the ninth [day of] the [Jewish month of] Av." The Jewish month of Av takes place in midsummer (generally July-August). This was a day of fasting and mourning when the book of Lamentations was read since it recognized the destructions of the Jewish temple first by Babylon (586 BC) and then by Rome (AD 70).

But this day quickly evolved into something wider. It began to recall the many losses and tragedies that have befallen the Jews, including an attempted (and failed) uprising against Rome in AD 132–135. Today Tisha B'Av is celebrated widely in Israel. Almost a quarter of Israelis fast, and half of the people avoid all entertainment. Among orthodox Jews, on this one day they will not greet friends when passing them in the street. They are reliving sorrow and grief publicly.

© Eitan Simanor/Alamy

Children play with graggers and other noisemakers at a Purim festival in Jerusalem.

Another minor festival with greater antiquity is Purim (Heb. "Lots"), which occurs on the fourteenth day of the month of Adar (generally February-March). Here Jews studied the book of Esther and recalled the story of how a Persian prime minister (Haman) tried to destroy the Jewish people. (He cast "lots" to determine the day of the genocide.) A newly appointed Jewish queen named Esther, together with her cousin, Mordecai, revealed this plot to the king and all was reversed. Haman was killed (in a gallows intended for Mordecai, Esth. 7:10), and a decree protecting the Jewish people was published.

The Jewish oral law (the Mishnah) devotes a tractate to this called *Megillah*, which in Hebrew refers to "the scroll" or more precisely, "the scroll of Esther" (in Heb. *Megillat Esther*). This record tells us that this feast was recognized quite early. Today synagogues continue to recognize Purim, and their traditions are splendid. It is a day of feasting and joy—the very opposite of Tisha B'Av. During the reading of Esther in synagogues everyone makes noise. When Haman's name is mentioned (fifty-four times in the story), Jews will hiss and groan. Some will bring a noisemaker called a Purim "Gragger" (a Yiddish term). In Hebrew, it is called a *Ra'ashan* (from Heb. *ra'ash*, "noise"). These Purim noisemakers blot out the name of Haman as the story is being read.

JUDAISM AND HANUKKAH

We have one record that Jesus visited a minor festival of Judaism. However the gospel records are not exhaustive, and so we should not conclude he failed to celebrate others as well. Most of us would recognize the Festival of Hanukkah (sometimes spelled Chanukah), but few of us know its story. Jesus did. In fact, every Jewish child living in the first century knew the Hanukkah story intimately. However, this particular festival celebrated at the Jerrusalem temple was one of the least well-known festivals in the Jewish calendar. It was celebrated on the twenty-fifth day of the month of Kislev (usually November-December), and it lasted eight days. In many respects, it seems to have been built on the model of Tabernacles.

Hanukkah was never a biblical festival. It began in the second-century BC following a successful Jewish uprising against the Greeks who had occupied Jerusalem. But we do know it was celebrated in Jesus' day. The gospel of John refers to it (John 10:22, "the Festival of Dedication"), and it is men-

DREIDEL

PhotoDisc

HANUKKAH CHOCOLATES

tioned casually in the Mishnah (*Rosh Hashanah* 1:3; *Megillah* 3:4, 6) as well as in Jewish histories (I'll quote these sources shortly).

Since the conquest of Alexander the Great in 332 BC, Greek influence in the Middle East not only controlled the political aspirations of people like the Jews, but it gradually assimilated them into the Greek way of life. Within 150 years, Israel had adopted numerous Greek cultural and religious habits. Even the Hebrew Scriptures were translated into Greek for Jews who could no longer read Hebrew. Jewish resistance to this met opposition not only from Greeks but from Jews who had compromised their commitment both to Jewish culture and faith. Corrupt priests with names such as Jason and Menelaus contributed to the demise of Jewish temple worship.

In the 160s BC a notorious Greek ruler named Antiochus IV increased pressure on all minorities in his empire. He outlawed Jewish rituals such as circumcision, he burned Scripture scrolls, and he banned any Jewish festivals. Then in December of 167 he did something notorious: Greek priests sacrificed a pig on the holy altar of the temple and erected a pagan idol there. Pigs are unclean animals in Judaism, and so he intentionally desecrated the temple.

This inspired courageous Jewish leaders to begin a fight of

resistance. Its first leader, Judas Maccabeus (this was his nickname: Maccabeus means "hammer"), captured Jerusalem's temple and in 165 BC cleansed and rededicated the temple, restoring its worship. Hanukkah is a Hebrew word for "dedication," and it became the name of the winter festival in Jerusalem that remembered these events. Listen to the original—and indeed famous—words coming from a Jewish history book written perhaps a hundred years before Jesus. We can assume that Jesus read these stirring words regularly, which described Judas's retaking of the temple and its purification:

> Then Judas and his brothers said, "See, our enemies are crushed; let us go up to cleanse the sanctuary and dedicate it." So all the army assembled and they went up to Mount Zion. There they saw the sanctuary desolate, the altar profaned, and the gates burned. In the courts they saw bushes sprung up as in a thicket, or as on one of the mountains. They saw also the chambers of the priests in ruins. Then they tore their clothes and mourned with great lamentation; they sprinkled themselves with ashes and fell face down on the ground. And when the signal was given with the trumpets, they cried out to Heaven.
> Then Judas detailed men to fight against those in the citadel until he had cleansed the sanctuary. He chose blameless priests devoted to the law, and they cleansed the sanctuary and removed the defiled stones to an unclean place. They deliberated what to do about the altar of burnt offering, which had been profaned. And they thought it best to tear it down, so that it would not be a lasting shame to them that the Gentiles had defiled it. So they tore down the altar, and stored the stones in a convenient place on the temple hill until a prophet should come to tell what to do with them. Then they took unhewn [or uncut] stones, as the law directs, and built a new altar like the former one. They also rebuilt the sanctuary and the interior of the temple, and consecrated the courts. They made new holy vessels, and brought the lampstand, the altar of incense, and the table into the temple. Then they offered incense on the altar and lit the lamps on the lampstand, and these gave light in the temple. They placed the bread on the table and hung up the curtains. Thus they finished all the work they had undertaken. (1 Macc. 4:36–50 NRSV)

Note how Judas "dedicated" the cleansed temple. This "Festival of Dedication" celebrated the rededication of the temple in 164 BC after its defilement. Josephus in his *Antiquities* wrote to explain his faith to his Roman readers, and in an important chapter, he explains the feast and its origins. After telling the story of the victory of Judas, he tells us more. Here Josephus refers to the feast as the Festival of Lights:

They were so very glad at the revival of their customs, when after a long time of intermission, they unexpectedly had regained the freedom of their worship, that they made it a law for their posterity, that they should keep a festival, on account of the restoration of their temple worship, for eight days. And from that time to this we celebrate this festival, and call it Lights. I suppose the reason was, because this liberty beyond our hopes appeared to us; and that thence was the name given to that festival. (Ant. 12.324–25)

Later Jewish tradition (from about AD 600) expanded the symbolism of the festival by explaining more about the tradition of light. The legend said that when Judas looked for oil to light the candelabra in the temple, he found that the oil was useless and unclean. He could find only one oil jar that had been sealed correctly by a priest—but this was only enough to burn for one day. Miraculously the oil burned for eight days. This miracle has been commemorated ever since in the Hanukkah menorahs and their eight candles that burn in windows each winter in Jewish neighborhoods.[19]

Unlike the pilgrimage festivals, great crowds of pilgrims did not come to Jerusalem for Hanukkah. This was a festival recognized by the people but celebrated and studied in the temple among the priests. If the temple needed to be rededicated, Jerusalem's leaders asked: How did the temple become defiled in the first place? Why did Jewish priests collaborate with those who defiled it? How did leadership so desperately fail that military heroism was required to

A SMALL FLASK USED TO CONTAIN PERFUME OR OIL

Aryballos with chain, Roman, c. 100 AD by Freud Museum, London, UK/The Bridgeman Art Library

restore worship? Clearly the temple leaders in the second century BC had lost their way. And so many asked, How do we prevent them from losing their way again?

Among the biblical texts pondered during this season, Ezekiel 34 was central to every Hanukkah discussion. Throughout Israel's history, its leaders had always been known as shepherds. God was Israel's shepherd (Ps. 23; Isa. 40:9), but likewise men like Moses and David were skilled shepherds (Ex. 3:1; 1 Sam. 16:11) who went on to become great leaders. This led to the idea that "shepherding" and the care of sheep—feeding them, protecting them, caring for them—were excellent metaphors for what it meant to be a king. When Israel lived in times of disarray, they were "like sheep without a shepherd" (Num. 27:17; 1 Kings 22:17; cf. Matt. 9:36).

Ezekiel picked up the shepherd image dramatically and used it for the overwhelming failures of leadership during his generation. He wrote:

> The word of the LORD came to me: "Son of man, prophesy against the shepherds of Israel; prophesy and say to them: 'This is what the Sovereign LORD says: Woe to you shepherds of Israel who only take care of yourselves! Should not shepherds take care of the flock? You eat the curds, clothe yourselves with the wool and slaughter the choice animals, but you do not take care of the flock.'" (Ezek. 34:1–3)

MENORAH

PhotoDisc

GOD WAS ISRAEL'S SHEPHERD.

For Ezekiel, the consequences of these failures were severe. It meant that God was setting himself against the "shepherds" of Israel.

> Therefore, you shepherds, hear the word of the LORD: As surely as I live, declares the Sovereign LORD, because my flock lacks a shepherd and so has been plundered and has become food for all the wild animals, and because my shepherds did not search for my flock but cared for themselves rather than for my flock, therefore, you shepherds, hear the word of the LORD: This is what the Sovereign LORD says: I am against the shepherds and will hold them accountable for my flock. I will remove them from tending the flock so that the shepherds can no longer feed themselves. I will rescue my flock from their mouths, and it will no longer be food for them. (Ezek. 34:7–10)

Within a festival that considered the stunning lapses of Jewish leadership during the Greek era — an era when the temple had been profaned and desecrated and brave faithful Jews had to dedicate it once more to God's use — Ezekiel 34 brought a dramatic warning to leaders everywhere. Jesus knew this, and he took advantage of it one winter in Jerusalem.

JESUS AND HANUKKAH

The setting of John 10 is found in this festival of Hanukkah. It is a remarkable story because just a few months before this

SHEEPFOLD

festival, Jesus had engaged in running debates with the Jewish leadership of Jerusalem. In fact, the hostilities were so intense that these leaders tried to arrest him, but they failed (John 7:30). They even sent military officers to incarcerate him, but they were too impressed with him to do it (7:32). Some residents of Jerusalem had decided he was a prophet (7:40) and still others wondered if he was the Messiah (7:41). Clearly the authorities were angered by all of it.

Jesus had even challenged them by asking if they were *really* Abraham's children, given their attitudes (John 8:39) — and at one point he suggested that they were acting as if the devil was their father (8:44). To say the least, in the months just prior to Hanukkah, Jesus had been in severe debates. And it didn't help when he healed a blind man (John 9) and suggested that the truly blind in Jerusalem were those who were running the city (9:39).

When Jesus returned to Jerusalem after these conflicts, he took an opportunity to give a short sermon within the city — I imagine within earshot of the temple. And the theme? Jesus spoke about good shepherds, false shepherds, strangers, hired workers, and sheep as a poignant reminder to Israel's leaders about the legacy of leadership and its failings. He certainly had Ezekiel 34 on his mind.

I am the good shepherd. The good shepherd lays down his life for the sheep. The hired hand is not the shepherd and does not own the sheep. So when he sees the wolf coming, he abandons the sheep and runs away. Then the wolf attacks the flock and scatters it. (John 10:11 – 12)

The parallels with Ezekiel are obvious — but the dramatic discovery is that he was speaking these things at Hanukkah. In the very season that recalled the failure of Israel's shepherds under the Greeks, now Jesus stepped forward and assumed the heroic role of the season (Judas Maccabeus?).

But Jesus also developed the shepherd imagery significantly beyond Ezekiel. For Jesus, leadership was not a matter of simply making sure the sheep were tended (though this was assumed). Nor was it only about living honestly with them. For him, sincere shepherding meant nurturing, guiding, and knowing the sheep in a manner that was as intimate as it was heroic. If danger threatened the sheep, such a shepherd would run them into a wilderness sheepfold and stand at its entrance, placing himself between his sheep and wild animals. "The reason my Father loves me is that I lay down my life — only to take it up again" (10:17).[20]

The temple courtyard was surrounded on all sides by colonnaded porches that gave shelter from the weather. On the south, the temple had a massive "Royal Porch" with 160 five-

REMAINS OF THE COLUMNS FROM THE ROYAL PORCH, NOW DESTROYED AND FALLEN DOWN ON A FIRST-CENTURY STREET

ton columns holding up an expansive roof. (The columns were arrayed in four rows with forty columns per row.) Solomon's Porch was a narrower porch on the eastern edge of the temple courtyard overlooking the Kidron Valley. These porches were used by teachers as windbreaks during the winter months and sun shelters during summer. Jesus gave this remarkable Hanukkah exhortation in Solomon's Porch (John 10:22–23).

Following the speech, the old debates of the previous three months resurfaced immediately. But now they seem reduced to two central complaints. (1) Was Jesus claiming to be the Christ (or Messiah, John 10:24)? And if he was, how could he prove it? In Jesus' mind, the evidence of his identity was a settled affair and he would not argue the point (10:25–26). (2) Their second complaint was more severe. His opponents suspected that he was making claims that exceeded that of the Messiah. Was he claiming to be the Son of God as well? Or worse, was he making some divine claim for himself (10:33)? His famous statement, "I and the Father are one" (10:30), belongs here and certainly stunned his accusers.

These were the two central accusations that were crystallized at Hanukkah—but also became the focus of his interrogation during his trial the approaching spring (Luke 22:67, 70). Hanukkah brought the charges against Jesus to the fore in debate, and the coming Passover in a few months would bring those same charges to trial.

The leaders judged this sort of talk as blasphemy (John 10:31). But we need to hear Jesus' response carefully because it too is linked to this festival of Hanukkah. Jesus debated like a first-century rabbi. In his defense he first noted that the general use of "gods" was known in the Old Testament (Ps. 82), and it was used for those who were bearers of the Word of the Lord (John 10:34–35). Then he wondered aloud: Was not the Messiah at least this significant?

But he wanted to go further. To be the Messiah did mean more. If the first premise was correct, what do we say of him who is a *unique* vehicle of the Word of God—who is the Word itself (John 1:1)? Of course Psalm 82:6 does not mean that couriers of God are divine, but the presence of the term "god" alone was sufficient for Jesus to make his point the way rabbis typically did in that day.

In each of the festivals we have seen how Jesus deliberately took up one feature of the festival and used it for his own purposes. At Passover he was the bread of life. At Tabernacles he was the living water. These images each unveiled something of Jesus' person. But here only the most careful listeners would catch Jesus' subtlety. Remember how Hanukkah (or Dedication) recalled the cleansing and rededication of the temple. The ancient Jewish story said that Judas cleansed the "holy place" (Gk. *hagia*) and "dedicated" it (1 Macc. 4:36, 48). Here Jesus claimed that he had been "set apart" or "made holy" or "consecrated" (Gk. *hagiazô*). This was the same language used in the Hanukkah liturgies. If Hanukkah thought about the dedication of the "holy place" (*hagia*), what if the "holy one" (*hagios*) himself was standing in their midst? It is no accident that John's gospel again and again eagerly compares Jesus with the temple (1:14; 2:21). Here at Hanukkah a new temple, consecrated by God, had appeared.

FAITH AND HANUKKAH

Hanukkah was a festival that urged Jewish leaders to think about failed and successful leadership. It retold the stories of corruption under Greek occupation in order to press leaders in

Z. Radovan/www.BibleLandPictures.com

THIS WILDERNESS IS INHOSPITABLE, WHICH MEANS SHEPHERDS NEED TO TAKE SPECIAL CARE TO WATCH AND PROTECT THEIR SHEEP.

the present to weigh their ultimate commitments. Were they faithful? Just? Did they care for their people as a committed shepherd cared for his sheep?

Jesus' description of leadership-through-shepherding is a poignant reminder of what it must mean to be a leader among God's people today. It also reminds us that we are also sheep, and we need to recognize the true character of our Shepherd. Jesus portrays himself as a shepherd who is not only invested in his sheep, but knows them by name and will protect them despite the threats that come to them. I cannot underscore sufficiently the danger of leading a hundred sheep across the Judean wilderness two thousand years ago. Predators were everywhere, and a flock was an obvious target. Nevertheless Middle Eastern shepherds were famous for not only knowing their sheep well but also for protecting them at all costs.

During the Palestinian uprising in the late 1980s the Israeli army decided to punish a village near Bethlehem for not paying its taxes (which, the village claimed, simply financed their occupation). The officer in command rounded up all of the village animals and placed them in a large barbed-wire pen. Later in the week a woman approached him and begged him to release her flock, arguing that since her husband was dead, the animals were her only source of livelihood. He pointed to the pen with hundreds of animals and quipped that it was impossible because he could not find her animals. She asked that if she could in fact separate them herself, would he be willing to let her take them? He agreed. A soldier opened the gate and the woman's son produced a small reed flute. He played a simple tune again and again—and soon, sheep heads began popping up across the pen. The young boy continued his music and walked home followed by his flock of twenty-five sheep. *The boy knew his sheep—and his sheep knew him.*

This is precisely the image I need to retain. The wilderness is a desperate place. Life is a desperate place. Our shepherd is skilled and courageous. And if we remain under his leadership, if we recognize his voice, we will find safety and flourish.

Chapter 6

JESUS AND HIS FINAL PASSOVER

John 13–19

AS A faithful Jew living in the first century, Jesus celebrated Passover each year. He began doing this when he was just a child and no doubt continued throughout his life. It involved a walking trip of over a hundred miles south to Jerusalem and then a long stay there for eight days filled with feasting, dancing, song, renewed friendships, and worship at the temple. The festivities centered on the "Great Story" of Moses and Israel's liberation from Egypt. By the time Jesus was thirty, he could move through these ceremonies with ease. He had sacrificed many lambs. He likely knew how to roast them as well for the traditional Passover meal. And he understood intimately what each of these ceremonies meant.

While this was a regular routine of Jesus' life, the Gospels give us scant evidence of Jesus' own journeys to Jerusalem for the Passover Feast. I imagine they didn't feel the need to say more. Matthew, Mark, and Luke record only one Passover visit in his adult years. John's gospel records three Passover visits: John 2:13–25; John 6; and John 13–19. However, each gospel makes one idea crystal clear: Jesus was fully aware that his arrival in Jerusalem at this final Passover would end his life.

PASSOVER SEDER PLATE

LIKE ANY MAJOR CITY IN FESTIVAL TIME, JERUSALEM ANTICIPATED THE ARRIVAL OF THE SEASON WITH EXTENSIVE PREPARATIONS.

CEMETERY AREAS WERE CLEARLY MARKED SO THAT VISITORS WOULD NOT ACCIDENTALLY CONTRACT "CORPSE IMPURITY."

Along with his apostles he was walking (likely with other Galilee pilgrims) to Jerusalem to attend the feast, and all along he reminded them that when they arrived, he would be killed (Mark 8:31; 9:31; 10:33–34).

Jesus knew his opponents were planning to kill him. He also believed that this was a central part of his mission. But I am convinced that Jesus wanted to die during the Festival of Passover because of the profound meaning it would convey with regard to his sacrifice.

JERUSALEM PREPARATIONS

Like any major city in festival time, Jerusalem anticipated the arrival of the season with extensive preparations. The city would likely triple in size as Jewish pilgrims from Galilee to Rome arrived with money to spend and news to tell. Those with means would rent rooms within Jerusalem's city walls, but most camped on the surrounding hills.

HUGE CARVED STONES FROM HERODIAN ERA

Cemetery areas were clearly marked so that visitors would not accidentally contract "corpse impurity" and so have to enter a cleansing ceremony (using water and ashes) and miss the feast. Animals (both lambs and goats) that qualified for sacrifice were checked and double-checked for sale within the temple. And because of the many Roman coins in circulation (some of dubious value and others having offensive imperial images),

SILVER SHEKELS FROM TYRE

The Jewish Passover

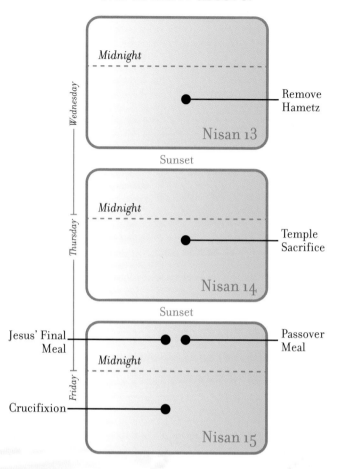

money changing began in earnest. Only silver shekels from Tyre were acceptable to the priests for payments.

The above diagram explains how the final days of the Passover season were celebrated. Note again that Jews in the first century marked their days from dusk to dusk (unlike our days, marked from midnight to midnight). There were twelve months of the year (see chapter 1 for their names), and within each month, the days were numbered. The Passover took place in the springtime month of Nisan, and its feast took place during the evening of Nisan 15. We recognize this as Thursday evening. But for Jews, that evening at dusk opened a new day (Nisan 15), and the day preceding dusk was a different "day" (Nisan 14). Note in the chart that Jesus celebrated his meal, was arrested, and was crucified all on the same Jewish "day." By modern reckoning, of course, he hosted this meal on Thursday evening and was crucified on Friday.

Because Passover included the Feast of Unleavened Bread (see chapter 2), first-century Jews in Jerusalem had to remove from their homes any *hametz* (or *chametz*) — that is, basically anything that used yeast. Everyone knew that the great meal would take place on the evening of Nisan 15. So from Nisan 13 to the afternoon of Nisan 14, the city was scoured (Mishnah, *Pesachim* 3:1). This included bread and especially beer (a beverage made with barley and yeast).

Two days before the feast (Nisan 13) there was a frantic search using lights to uncover even crumbs that might be hidden behind shelves. You could either eat what you found, burn it, toss it to the wind, feed it to cattle, or sell it to non-Jews (Mishnah, *Pesachim* 2:1). But everything had to be finished by midday before the meal when the lambs were slaughtered. As the ancient Israelites in Egypt ate a meal with unleavened bread (Ex. 12:8), so too, Jerusalem would be ready to do the same.

Families would generally group together for the celebration of the feast. While they may have been camping on Jerusalem's hills, they were required to eat the meal within the city walls.

Z. Radovan/www.BibleLandPictures.com

BURNING THE *HAMETZ* IN JERUSALEM FOR THE PREPARATION OF PASSOVER

CHAPTER SIX, JESUS AND HIS FINAL PASSOVER

MODEL OF EGYPTIAN
MAN BREWING BEER

This meant finding a room or courtyard for use inside Jerusalem. And it meant locating an acceptable animal that was healthy, young, and without blemish—if you didn't bring your own.

From about 4:00 to 6:00 p.m. (the ninth to the eleventh hours of Nisan 14), lambs were brought to the temple in three waves of worshipers to bring order to the congestion (Mishnah, *Pesachim* 5:5). All Levites and priests were ready for work. The Levites—hundreds of men—would begin singing the Hallel Psalms (Pss. 113–118) as thousands of lamps held by their owners lined up in the temple courts. When all was ready for the sacrifice, a priest would take up a *shofar* (a ram's horn) and blow three loud blasts to signal the beginning of the sacrificial work. Lambs were killed by cutting the throat so that the blood could be caught and drained. But the serving Levite or priest also needed to be assured that the lamb was alive and acceptable. The "spurting" blood from the lamb was one verification that life was being sacrificed for life.

If we expect that twenty people might consume the lamb and if 100,000 people were in Jerusalem, that meant that five thousand lambs were slain on Nisan 14. According to other estimates, if Jerusalem had a population of 100,000 and ten persons slaughtered one lamb, then perhaps 10,000 lambs were killed. This has led many to wonder how it happened. Jeru-

BARLEY WAS COMMONLY USED
IN BOTH BREAD AND BEER.

salem had a roster of thousands of priests, who likely set up stations in the outer courtyards of the temple to service the public.

Once the lamb was killed, its blood was caught in a basin, which was passed back until it was spilled at the base of the altar. After each successive wave of sacrifices, the altar was washed down. The carcass was then hung on a hook on the temple walls, it was partially cleaned, its fleece was stripped off, and it was returned to the Israelite worshipers so they could then return it to their waiting family for roasting.

SHOFAR

The entire scene must have been remarkable. The city was filled with the noise of the lambs, their cry at the slaughter, the loud singing of large male choirs, the echo of *shofar* blasts, and the smell of roasted meat from every corner of the city. To do this each year for your life (from

Karim Kadim/AP Images

MUSLIM MEN SLAUGHTER SHEEP ON THE FIRST
DAY OF *EID UL-FITR* IN BAGHDAD, IRAQ.

childhood) left indelible memories unifying Israel to its Great
Story of Moses and the exodus.

There is probably only one comparable ceremony left in
the Middle East today that matches this. Muslims celebrate
a month of fasting called Ramadan, and this is concluded by
a major feast called *Eid* (Arab *Eid ul-Fitr*). On the morning of
Eid, sheep, goats, and young camels are sacrificed for the feast
throughout cities such as Amman and Damascus. This does not
happen only in butcher stores as we'd expect, but it happens
everywhere. The audible sound of thousands of dying animals is
something a Westerner will never forget if you happen to be in
a Muslim city on *Eid*. But it was commonplace to people in the
ancient Middle East, particularly in Jerusalem.

JESUS AND THE MEAL

When Jesus came to Jerusalem during his final week, it was the
season of Passover (Mark 14:1 – 2; John 13:1). He traveled from
Galilee to the oasis at Jericho, then climbed the mountains
west from there until he came to Jerusalem. The Roman road
he took is still visible today in those hills. He remained with
friends in Bethany (Mark 11:1; 14:3) since this was only a short
walk over the Mount of Olives to the city.

Remains of the Roman road above Jericho

On "Palm Sunday" he crossed the Mount of Olives riding a donkey, descended the hill, and was met by thousands of cheering crowds waving palm branches—a common symbol of Jewish nationalism. These people were no doubt Galilee pilgrims camped around the city for Passover, and they recognized him. His arrival began about five days of intense debates with the leadership of Jerusalem. But as the week wore on, his popularity began to swell as quickly as the hostility of the temple leaders. Mark records that the temple leaders were seeking a way to arrest him "by stealth" and kill him quickly. But they were reluctant because of the crowds of people packed into Jerusalem for the feast (Mark 14:2).

Jesus, of course, was eager to complete the week with his own Passover meal, and this required finding a location inside the walled city. But he did not want it to be the venue for his arrest.

Bar Kokhba coin showing palm branches

BASIN USED TO WASH FEET BEFORE
ENTERING A RITUAL BATH

He located the room inside the city privately and then assigned two of his apostles to enter the city, find a man "carrying water" (this was a signal since men rarely did this), and follow him to the room to prepare the meal (Mark 14:13–16). We have to assume that it was then Nisan 14, and one of the preparations required of these men was to complete the Passover sacrifice at the temple. Jesus and the others would then meet them later.[21]

Two important events occurred in the room where Jesus hosted this meal. First, John 13 says that Jesus washed his disciples' feet. This was a remarkable and stunning act of servanthood, where Jesus not only showed his own service to them, but also modeled what he expected of their behavior in the future. But this may also be linked to Passover. Tradition required that Jews participating in the feast be in a *state of purity* just like that of the Levites (or priestly assistants). This means that if a person was in an unclean state (from corpse impurity, bodily discharges, or Gentile contact), they had to wash in a ritual bath.

On the one hand, the foot washing may be simply the common act of welcoming well-known in this culture. On the other hand, there may be more. When Peter refused to be washed, Jesus told him that this deed wasn't voluntary but mandatory if he wanted to be a part of Christ (John 13:8). Peter impulsively asked to be washed from head to foot, which was *precisely* what Passover purity required. Jesus then explained that what he was doing would make them clean all over (13:10), but that only "later" would they understand the deeper meaning of this purity. In other words, talk of purity and washing surrounded the moments before the meal, and this is exactly what Jesus would provide through his death on the cross.

Although the Gospels do not say so, we must assume that Jesus (or one of his followers) sacrificed an animal that day, it had been roasted, and a proper Passover was set before them. Eating a meal was fellowship in this culture. This is why Israelite altars were places that cooked the sacrifice (and seasoned it) so that when it was burned up, the "meal" was shared with God and reconciliation or fellowship was achieved. Such sacrifices were then consumed so that the worshiper participated in the "altar." At Passover, however, not everyone could participate that day in the offering of the lamb. Therefore it was understood: *those who ate the meat of the sacrificial victim shared in the benefits of its death.* You then became a "partner at the altar." Within the Passover rituals, eating the ritual elements of the meal was essential to participation.

This is the backstory when Jesus picked up bread and broke it, identifying it with his upcoming sacrifice. He poured wine and referred to it as his blood poured out. He then invited them to eat the bread and drink the wine — and using the context of Passover, we see that he was inviting them to become partners with him at his altar, the cross. In a sacrificial meal, he was now providing a new sacrifice, a

JESUS WASHING THE FEET OF THE APOSTLES IN AN ALTAR PAINTING (AD 1400/1420) FROM MAINZ, GERMANY

Wikimedia Commons

Passover sacrifice, and his life was going to be a new lamb killed during this day of sacrifice.

The traditional meal was organized around four cups of (real) red wine (Mishnah, *Pesachim* 10:1), which were diluted with water (the Greeks thought that drinking undiluted wine was barbaric). In fact, all Mediterranean cultures cultivated and treasured good wine. Thucydides, the fifth-century Greek historian, once famously wrote, "The peoples of the Mediterranean began to emerge from barbarism when they learned to cultivate the olive and the vine." Jews were no different. At Passover even the poor were expected to have all four full cups. Later Jewish tradition has given names to these, but it is uncertain if these reflect names used in antiquity. The first may have been the *Kiddush* (or cup of holiness), the second the *Maggid* (for telling of the Passover

CARVING SHOWS JESUS BREAKING BREAD AT THE LAST SUPPER, FROM WESTERN GERMANY (AD 1420/30).

EARLY FIRST-CENTURY BRONZE DRINKING CUP

Baker Photo Archive

Kim Walton, courtesy of the British Museum

story), the third the *Birkat Hamazon* (for blessings), and the fourth the *Hallel* (for praise).

Many scholars suspect that Jesus used the third cup for his sacrificial dedication. In an odd passage, Paul casually refers to the Christian celebration of this meal, and he names the cup of the Christian "Lord's Supper" as the "cup of thanksgiving" (1 Cor. 10:16). There is one reason why this is fascinating, because Jesus then told his apostles that he would not drink again of the "fruit of the vine" until he did so in the kingdom of God (Mark 14:25). He then dismissed the meal after they sang a song, and they departed for the Mount of Olives.

This opens an inevitable question: Did Jesus never complete the meal? Did he not permit the drinking of the final cup (perhaps the Praise or *Hallel* cup)? And if this was intentional, it means that Jesus left his followers (ourselves included) in a suspended Passover liturgy that can only be completed when we join Christ in heaven. Much of this notion is speculative, and it is only Paul's inadvertent tip that may give it away. But it may explain why Christians from the beginning thought that this meal needed to hallmark their life together. Jesus not only requested its repetition ("do this in remembrance of me"), but

© 1995 by Phoenix Data Systems

THE PEOPLES OF THE MEDITERRANEAN BEGAN TO EMERGE FROM BARBARISM WHEN THEY LEARNED TO CULTIVATE THE OLIVE AND THE VINE.

CHAPTER SIX, JESUS AND HIS FINAL PASSOVER

THE EASTERN CITY GATE OF JERUSALEM

his followers understood that within the life of this sacred meal, they would discover the hidden meaning of Jesus' life and work.

Jews commonly spent the balance of that night in prayer, and it was common practice to distribute gifts to the poor. The city gates of Jerusalem were left open that night, and there was a lot of coming and going. This explains why Jesus entered an olive grove in a valley just east of Jerusalem, beneath the

OLIVE TREES IN THE GARDEN OF GETHSEMANE

city walls, and there decided to pray with his disciples (Mark 14:32–42). He was living out an age-old Passover tradition. This also explains why he was found in that same grove late the same night. This place (called "Gethsemane," which means "olive oil press") would become the site of his arrest. Beneath these trees, Jesus would be "handed over" just like a Passover lamb who was earlier sacrificed the same day.

JESUS AND THE CROSS

The themes of Passover not only surrounded the events of Jesus' final meal, but they also became a vital part of his suffering and death. In fact, it would be impossible to understand Jesus' death in its fullest if we did not know how Passover images were at play.

We have seen that the Thursday evening meal and the events of Friday each lived within the same Jewish "day" called Nisan 15. Therefore when Jesus was interrogated by the high priest Friday morning, met with a full session of the high council (or Sanhedrin), and was transferred to the Roman governor Pontius Pilate, *it was still Passover.* John 18:28 reminds us that the Jewish leaders were apprehensive about entering Pilate's headquarters lest they be defiled for the Passover.

Therefore when Jesus was tortured and crucified that same afternoon, *it continued to be Passover.* The reason the women were eager to have his body placed in a tomb was because on this particular year, the Sabbath day was going to follow Passover; and once dusk broke over Jerusalem on Friday, it would be impossible to tend to his body appropriately. (As it was, the women did not complete his burial preparations and therefore Jesus remained in his tomb until Sunday morning, when the women planned to return to complete their work.)

But the Passover imagery does not end in the upper room. The Gospels—and in particular the gospel of John—are careful to remind us that Jesus was not only celebrating Passover, *he had become a Passover sacrifice.* He was the lamb of God (the Passover lamb),[22] who would take away the sin of the world. In John 19:28–30 we learn that Jesus was thirsty on the cross. Here no doubt Jesus is thinking of the great lament of Psalm 22, a psalm of death and anguish he likely recited from the cross.

But to assuage his thirst, some soldiers (or other bystanders) took a sponge, filled it with wine (it was wine-vinegar, diluted with water commonly used among soldiers), and offered it to him. The Greek record of this is uncertain: either the sponge was placed on a Roman javelin (Gk. *hyssos*) or on a branch of hyssop (Gk. *hyssôpos*). Most scholars think John had hyssop in mind because this was the plant used in the Egyptian Passover to mark the Jewish homes with lamb's blood (Ex. 12:22). Hyssop was also used frequently in temple sacrifice ceremonies (Lev. 14:4, 6, 49, 51). Here, then, at the cross appears one of the famed instruments of the Passover story.

But there is more. When Jesus was on the cross, the soldiers decided to expedite his death (the Jewish historian Josephus recalls many crucifixions that lasted days), and the customary method for this was by breaking the legs of the crucified victims. The legs would fracture and the person would either bleed out or asphyxiate since they no longer could hold themselves upright. The soldiers broke the legs of the other two victims, but when they came to Jesus he was already dead—and so he was left alone. Now why does John record this note? He tells us in John 19:36. The Passover sacrifice could not have any

AT JESUS' CRUCIFIXION, THE SOLDIERS USED A JAVELIN TO PIERCE JESUS TO CONFIRM HIS DEATH; WHEN THEY DID, BOTH "BLOOD AND WATER" FLOWED FROM HIS SIDE.

THE CAPER PLANT, ALSO CALLED HYSSOP

broken bones and during the meal itself, a Jew could not break a bone of the animal (Ex. 12:5, 46; 29:1; Num. 9:12; *Jub.* 49:13). Even Psalm 34:20 may be in mind: the righteous sufferer will have none of his bones broken. Therefore Jesus fully qualified as a Passover sacrifice.

During these last minutes, the soldiers also used a javelin to pierce Jesus to confirm his death (John 19:34); when they did, both "blood and water" flowed from his side. Scholars have debated the meaning of these words for generations.[23] But an important Passover allusion may be at hand. For a lamb to qualify as a sacrifice, blood must *flow* from its body when it is slain (thus proving that it is a living sacrifice). Here again, Jesus is a living sacrifice, a qualified Passover victim whose life now is being poured out for the sake of those who follow him.

PASSOVER AND FAITH

One of the chief difficulties we have when we read the Gospels is that we do not have the repertoire of images that were instinctive for a Jew living two thousand years ago. We read about hyssop or we celebrate the Lord's Supper, and we do not have an immediate understanding of how these elements fit into the larger cycle of Jewish festivals.

Take one more example. When we read that water and blood flowed from Jesus' side on the cross, some Jews might think immediately about the plague in Egypt when Moses turned the Nile to blood after striking it with his rod (Ex. 7:15 – 21). Or they might think of the rock in the wilderness that Moses struck (Ex. 17:6; Num. 20:11). *Is Jesus that struck rock?* Paul delights in comparing Jesus to that rock (1 Cor. 10:4), and a later Jewish tradition (which we cannot date) says more: Moses struck the rock twice according to Numbers 20, once it flowed blood, the second time water.[24] When Jesus thus bleeds blood and water on the cross, are there symbols here that have escaped us?

We must not be averse to finding symbolism within our Scriptures because within these allusions to the rich festival tradition we may find unexpected meanings. In this case, Jesus ended his life at Passover. And he used the festival to help us understand the deeper meaning of his death. *He was a lamb sacrificed for the salvation of God's people.*

But I also enjoy the idea that Jesus in some manner interrupted his final Passover meal. If he ended the meal abruptly and never completed the four-cup sequence of the Jewish liturgy ("I will not drink again from the fruit of the vine until that day when I drink it new in the kingdom of God," Mark 14:25), he has left each of us within the church living in a suspended Passover season. In this sense, the church lives within Passover, continually celebrating the meal that lives at the center of its worship and anticipating the moment when we join Christ in heaven and drink the final cup — the cup of praise and rejoicing, the *Hallel* cup — with him.

Chapter 7

THE EARLY CHRISTIANS AND THE JEWISH FESTIVALS

Acts 1–2; Hebrews 9–10

WHENEVER MUSLIMS convert to Christianity, a part of them longs for the Islamic traditions and celebrations they've known from childhood. I understand that. It may be the Muslim new year that arrives in the month of Muharram or the dramatic month of fasting in the ninth month of Ramadan (followed by the great feast of *Eid ul-Fitr*). The same would be true of Christians who converted to the Muslim faith. They would always yearn to celebrate Christmas and Easter no matter what the local mosque was doing. No Muslim holiday can replace them.

I can imagine the same would be true for a Jew who newly joined the church; he or she would begin to pine for the traditions of Judaism. Messianic Jews recognize this and creatively wed Christian faith to Jewish tradition in order to satisfy that yearning. Passover is celebrated—but with Christian elements

PENTECOST FRESCO BY GIOTTO DI BONDONE (1266–1336), SCROVEGNI CHAPEL, PADUA, ITALY

and meanings. These communities are living between two traditions, and inevitably echoes of the ancient legacies will begin to emerge.

Certainly the early church understood this as well. The first believers in Jesus were Jews who had recently decided to follow Jesus as the Messiah. Once they did, they were forced to rethink the major categories of their Jewish faith. *Should they worship at the temple? Should they continue to offer sacrifices? Was Sabbath observance still an obligation? And what about the major festivals that punctuated the year?* Then there were the personal traditions. *Should we still circumcise our sons?* The pages of the New Testament give us some hints that these traditions were swirling around these earliest Christian communities and forcing them to rethink Christian faith through them.

This is probably why the Gospels give the attention they do to these Jewish festivals as well as the Sabbath. The Gospels were Christian Scriptures that helped the early Christians to understand their own faith and experience. So when Jesus expressed considerable freedom with regard to the Sabbath, this signaled a parallel freedom among those who first read those stories. Furthermore, these Christians began to see their own Christian experiences *through* these festivals. For instance, when Christ died on the cross, the truest meaning of this crisis-turned-blessing was found in the Festival of Passover and the Jewish Day of Atonement.

There are references to Jewish festivals later in the New Testament that still hold meaning for us today. Through them we see that the earliest church was coming to terms with its own life and faith as it forged a new world of uniquely Christian celebrations loosely moored to the traditions of Judaism.

PENTECOST

In chapter 1 we saw that Judaism held three great pilgrimage festivals: Passover (*Pesach*), Pentecost (*Shavuot*), and Tabernacles (*Sukkoth*). These three were based not only on the agricultural rhythms of the year, but also they served to tell the story of Israel's salvation. Israel was rescued from Egypt (Passover, *Pesach*), Israel met God at Mount Sinai (Pentecost, *Shavuot*), and then Israel wandered in the wilderness (Tabernacles, *Sukkoth*).

Kim Walton

JEWS CELEBRATING *SHAVOUT*, THE FEAST OF WEEKS.
PAUL MARKED TIME WITH COMMON JEWISH FESTIVALS.

The festivals provided an opportunity to reflect on each of these steps. But the agricultural cycles were in play as well: the start of the springtime cereal harvest (*Pesach*), the end of the cereal harvest along with sifting and milling (*Shavuot*), and the harvest of tree and vine (*Sukkoth*).

The Gospels refer to Passover and Tabernacles, but never to Pentecost (even though we can be sure Jesus recognized it). Too often Christians think of Pentecost as a Christian event. It was not. It was a Jewish feast that was casually recognized by Christian leaders such as Paul. Luke writes: "Paul had decided to sail past Ephesus to avoid spending time in the province of Asia, for he was in a hurry to reach Jerusalem, if possible, by the day of Pentecost" (Acts 20:16). Paul also tells the Corinthians that he will "stay on at Ephesus until Pentecost" (1 Cor. 16:8). This is Paul thinking like a Jew, marking time with a common festival.

Acts 2 records a fascinating reference to Pentecost (2:1). Seven weeks had passed since Jesus was crucified (recall that Pentecost/*Shavuot* takes place fifty days after the offering of the first barley sheaf of Passover, Lev. 23:16). The crowds had again returned to Jerusalem. All of Israel was in a state of fasting. And in this setting God overwhelmed and filled about 120 people (including the apostles) with the Holy Spirit. On the day of

PENTECOST, FROM THE
"HUNTERIAN PSALTER,"
c. 1170 AD

Pentecost, Peter offered the first sermon of Christian history (Acts 2:14–36). In response, three thousand people decided to follow Christ and join the fledgling community of Christians (Acts 2:41).

Pentecost was also called the Feast of Weeks, or in some cases the Day of Firstfruits (Heb. *Yom Habikkurim*). Since it was a celebration of the harvest, two fresh loaves of bread from the season's first cereal harvest were brought to the temple and offered to God in sacrifice (Lev. 23:15–21) along with a variety of other sacrifices (Num. 28:26–31). The worshiper then used Deuteronomy 26:1–11 as an affirmation of faith. When the basket of bread was handed to the priest, he listened for this confession: "I declare today to the LORD [our] God that I have come to the land the LORD swore to our ancestors to give us" (26:3). The priest would then set the basket at the base of the altar while the worshiper recited the history of his faith:

> *"My father was a wandering Aramean, and he went down into Egypt with a few people and lived there and became a great nation, powerful and numerous. But the Egyptians mistreated us and made us suffer, subjecting us to harsh labor. Then we cried out to the LORD, the God of our ancestors, and the LORD heard our voice and saw our misery, toil and oppression. So the LORD brought us out of Egypt with a mighty hand and an outstretched arm, with great terror and with signs and wonders. He brought us to this place and gave us this land, a land flowing with milk and honey; and now I bring the firstfruits of the soil that you, LORD, have given me." Place the basket before the LORD your God and bow down before him. (Deut. 26:5–10)*

In the New Testament period, Pentecost was taking on its fuller meaning. Now the temple reflected on the second stage of Israel's salvation, when God had met his people at Sinai and gave them the law. A valuable source that confirms this rethinking of Pentecost is an imaginative Jewish retelling of early Jewish history called the book of *Jubilees*, written a hundred years before Jesus. (Its Hebrew original only survives in Ethiopic and Latin; however, Hebrew portions now have been found among the Dead Sea Scrolls.) In this work Pentecost was viewed as a time of covenant renewal. This feast recalled the work of Moses in giving the law (*Jub.* 1:1–26) as well as the covenants given to Noah and Abraham (6:1, 10–11; 15:1–16). But this feast also charged every Israelite not simply to remember the law but to return to faithfulness (6:17). Centuries later Jewish rabbis declared that Exodus 19 (the giving of the law) should be read during Pentecost (Babylonian Talmud, *Megillah* 31a).[25]

This is fascinating to Christians because of one connection. If the Jewish feast of Pentecost was emerging in New Testament times as the occasion to recall the birth of Israel's covenant life under the law, for the church Pentecost became the day on which to recall the birth of the church under the power of the Spirit. As Israel was "born" on Pentecost, so too the church was "born" on Pentecost, inasmuch as it received the endowment

Todd Bolen/www.BiblePlaces.com

GATHERING WHEAT AT THE FEAST OF WEEKS

that would empower its ongoing life. Paul regularly contrasts law and Spirit; for him, this is the primary distinction between life in the church and life in Judaism (Gal. 3:2). He writes, "But if you are led by the Spirit, you are not under the law" (5:18). Pentecost is the birthday of God's people, when new relationships are forged and those people move either into the desert (Exodus-Numbers) or into the world (Acts).[26]

THE DAY OF ATONEMENT

Perhaps the most solemn festival in the Jewish year took place each autumn, five days before the Festival of Tabernacles (on the tenth day of the Jewish month Tishri). This was not a pilgrimage festival and so large crowds did not gather at the Jerusalem temple. It was the only time in the Hebrew Scriptures where God's people were called to fast. On the evening following Tishri 9, all Israel wherever they lived were called on to fast, think of their sins, and seek God for forgiveness. The fast would end at dusk following Tishri 10, giving a twenty-four-hour day of rest parallel to the Sabbath. On this day "eating, drinking, washing, anointing (with oils), putting on sandals, and marital intercourse are forbidden" (Mishnah, *Yoma* 8:1). It was such a serious task that the people were warned that those who refused to practice the Day of Atonement would perish (Lev. 23:29–30).

THE HIGH PRIEST WOULD DRESS IN SIMPLE WHITE LINEN ROBES (SETTING ASIDE HIS USUAL EXQUISITE HIGH PRIESTLY ATTIRE) TO BEGIN SACRIFICING A BULL FOR HIMSELF AND THE TEMPLE PRIESTHOOD.

Mary Evans Picture Library

MODEL OF A HIGH PRIEST IN
HIS USUAL CLOTHING

The Old Testament provides us with the details (Lev. 16 and 23). While the nation was fasting and praying, remarkably complicated sacrificial ceremonies were taking place in the temple (Lev. 16:1–28). The high priest—the chief officiant—had been set aside for days to ensure his perfect purity. He then sacrificed to make pure the structures of the temple: its walls, its altars, its sacred objects, and its curtains. Then after a ceremonial bath (for ritual purity), he dressed in simple white linen robes (setting aside his usual exquisite high priestly attire) to begin sacrificing a bull for himself and the temple priesthood.

Once this was completed, he took live coals in a censer from the altar of sacrifice along with two handfuls of incense and carried them into the Most Holy Place inside the temple—a place forbidden to all but him. Here he sprinkled the incense over the coals and filled the space with a cloud of incense smoke and sprinkled some of the blood of the sacrificed bull on the top (called "the mercy seat," KJV; "the atonement cover," NIV) of the only object in the Most Holy Place: the ark of the covenant.

After this the priest repeated the process, this time sacrificing a male goat for the sins of the people. Another incense cloud filled the inner sanctuary, and the goat blood was sprinkled again on the mercy seat. Finally, he mixed the blood of the goat with the blood of the bull and placed this on the great altar of burned sacrifice in the outer court. This made all of the instruments of the temple pure for sacrifice to cover the sins of the people (Lev. 16:19).

But then came the most fascinating act. The priest took a second live goat, laid his hands on its head, and "confess[ed] over it all the wickedness and rebellion of the Israelites." This goat (the "scapegoat," Lev. 16:26) was then driven out into the eastern wilderness to show that God had driven Israel's sins away permanently (16:20–22). Remember: throughout this day while the priest was doing his work, all Israel was fasting and praying, participating thoughtfully (we might say) in the work of atonement transpiring in the temple.

This ceremony remained unchanged in the era of Jesus with but a few exceptions. Josephus (*J.W.* 5:219) and the Mishnah (*Yoma* 5:2) tell us that the Most Holy Place was empty since no doubt the ark had never been recovered following the Babylonian exile. Only the stone on which the ark rested remained, and so the priest rested the incense censer and sprinkled the blood on this stone. The Mishnah also explains that dozens of priests assisted in cleansing the temple altar and sacrificing animals; these assignments were distributed by lottery because on one occasion two priests fought over a task, and one fell off the altar and broke his leg (*Yoma* 2:2)!

DURING THE JEWISH CEREMONY OF SOLEMN EXPIATION, A HIGH PRIEST DRAWS LOTS FOR TWO GOATS, AND THE SCAPEGOAT IS SENT OUT INTO THE DESERT TO ATONE FOR THEIR SINS.

The two goats were brought to the high priest for inspection before the ceremonies. He used two red wool threads to distinguish them: the goat for sacrifice had a thread tied around his neck; the goat for the wilderness had the thread tied around his horns. During the ceremonies the scapegoat was presented to the high priest, and he laid his hands over the animal and prayed:

> O God, your people, the House of Israel, have committed iniquity, transgressed and sinned before you. O God, forgive, I pray, the iniquities and transgressions and sins which your people, the House of Israel, have committed and transgressed and sinned before you; as it is written in the law of your servant Moses, "For on this day shall atonement be made for you to cleanse you: from all your sins shall you be clean before the Lord (Leviticus 16:30)." (Mishnah, Yoma 6:2)

The priests and the people responded by bowing down with their faces to the ground and saying, "Blessed be the name of the glory of his kingdom for ever and ever!"

When the scapegoat was sent into the wilderness, the crowd assembled at the temple then cried out, "Bear our sins and be gone! Bear our sins and be gone!" (Yoma 6:4). Select nonpriestly men then drove the goat over the Mount of Olives east of Jerusalem and deep into the wilderness.

Imagine being a new Jewish Christian living in Jerusalem in about AD 45, about fifteen years after the ministry of Jesus. The rich ceremonies of the temple are continuing, and on the Day of Atonement you and your family wonder: *Should we not fast? Should we not participate in the great sacrifice for sin? If we neglect these ceremonies will our sins be covered?* The ache of these questions must have been enormous. We have firm evidence in the New Testament that Jewish Christians after Christ's death were wondering if they should return to their ancient sacrificial festivals.

The book of Hebrews was written to answer these questions. In a word, it was penned to warn Jewish Christians not to lapse back into Judaism as if such ceremonies and festivals would provide a more assured salvation. In Hebrews 9 – 10 we find a full description of the temple ceremonies and a remarkable Christian critique: *Jesus is our high priest* (Heb. 9:11). Hebrews contrasts the ongoing (and futile) efforts of the high priests,

A mosaic from the Kykkos Monastery on Cyprus. The sacrifice on Golgotha outweighs all previous sacrifices.

who annually bring the blood of bulls and goats into the inner sanctuary, with Jesus, who brought *his own blood* into a heavenly sanctuary, namely, the true house of God. Therefore, because the content of his sacrifice was superior (the cross, 9:12–14) and the venue of its offering superior (a heavenly temple, 9:24), Jesus has secured for us an "eternal redemption" for all time (9:12).

Thus Hebrews concludes: Why look to the Day of Atonement in Jerusalem when Jesus has accomplished an eternal work that makes all earthly works obsolete? Hebrews 8:6 is a good summary: "But in fact the ministry Jesus has received is as superior to theirs as the covenant of which he is mediator is superior to the old one, since the new covenant is established on better promises."

It was a bold step. Hebrews announces the obsolescence of the Day of Atonement for Jewish Christians who thought that their lives needed the supplement of more sacrifices in Jerusalem. These Jewish Christians were also being persecuted for their failure to abide by religious custom (Heb. 10:32–39). Returning to temple sacrifices would have lessened their sufferings. Hebrews, however, presses them to remain steadfast.

Christ was sufficient. One day on Golgotha outweighed count-less complex sacrifices on Tishri 10 that had been going on for centuries.

SABBATH

We have already seen that Jesus respected the Sabbath and made it his custom to go to the synagogue each Sabbath (Luke 4:16; see chapter 2). Not only is this a Jewish tradition, but we also have the fourth commandment, telling us to "remember the Sabbath day by keeping it holy" (Ex. 20:8). The Sabbath (Heb. *Shabbat*, derived from *shavat*, "rest") was a day to cease labor at the end of the week (the seventh day); on it Jews com-monly came to the synagogue for study and prayer, joined in communal meals, and reflected on God's Sabbath rest in Gen-esis 1. Paul observed the Sabbath (Acts 13:14, 44; 16:13; 18:4), and we may easily conclude that most early Christians did too.

But early on Christians abandoned this practice. Scholars have worked hard to reconstruct when this happened and why, but the basic explanations may be simple. Sabbath-keeping (along with circumcision) was one of the most prominent public markers of Judaism in the Roman Empire. As Gentiles increasingly joined the church, particularly under Paul's min-istry, these new converts saw no more reason to observe the Sabbath than they did to circumcise their sons. When Jewish and Gentile Christians first worked out their differences in Acts 15, not even James included Sabbath-keeping as one of his expectations for Gentile faithfulness. You can hear Paul work-ing this out when he writes to the Roman Christians:

> *One person considers one day more sacred than another; another considers every day alike. Each of them should be fully convinced in their own mind. Whoever regards one day as special does so to the Lord. Who-ever eats meat does so to the Lord, for they give thanks to God; and who-ever abstains does so to the Lord and gives thanks to God.* (Rom. 14:5–6)

Paul even has to defend Gentile Christians who are being criticized for not keeping the Sabbath. To the Colossians he writes: "Therefore do not let anyone judge you by what you eat or drink, or with regard to a religious festival, a New Moon celebration or a Sabbath day" (Col. 2:16). When the Galatians seemed to be slipping back into what they thought was Jewish piety by using circumcision, Paul seeks to dissuade them and continues further, "You are observing special days and months and seasons and years!" (Gal. 4:10). For Paul, adopting Jewish rituals because it may provide spiritual benefit is simply a mistake.

There are a few references to Christians gathering on the first day of the week in the New Testament, but it is unclear that this was a declared day of Christian worship. In 1 Corinthians 16:2 Paul mentions putting aside money on this day, but that is all we read. Revelation 1:10 refers to John being in the Spirit in "the Lord's Day," but knowing what it means is almost impossible. In the New Testament era (prior to AD 75 or 85) no publicly declared use of Sunday seems to exist.

In the late first century, tensions between Jews and Christians were acute, and a creed used in synagogues designed to flush out Jewish Christians (called the *Birkat Haminim*) may have contributed to Christians in the Roman era looking for new ways to identify themselves.[27] Many likely began meeting on Saturday nights—a practice that Roman emperors later deemed illegal—and this evolved into Sunday gatherings (recall that Saturday night was linked to Sunday in Jewish reckoning). We have no evidence that early Christians were equating Sunday with their version of the Sabbath but instead began to see this celebration as a way to hallmark the resurrection of Jesus (which took place on Sunday). It isn't until about seventy years after the death of Christ that Christians began thinking theologically about Sunday gatherings in earnest. The most important reference comes in the late first century by a nonbiblical document called *The Teaching of the Twelve Apostles* (Gk. *Didache*). Here we have perhaps the earliest description of what Christians did on their distinctive worship day.

> On the Lord's own day gather together and break bread and give thanks, having first confessed your sins so that your sacrifice may be pure. But let no one who has a quarrel with a companion join you until they have been reconciled, so that your sacrifice may not be defiled. For this is the sacrifice concerning which the Lord said, "In every place and time offer me a pure sacrifice, for I am a great king, says the Lord, and my name is marvelous among the nations." (Didache 14:1–3, Lightfoot trans.)

A bishop in Syria, Ignatius of Antioch, lived in the late first century as well and wrote the same things, even criticizing Sabbath observance as "antiquated" and arguing that keeping "the Lord's Day" is valuable because it celebrates Christ's resurrection through which Christians find life (Ignatius, *Letter to the Magnesians* 9:1).

IGNATIUS OF ANTIOCH

No doubt by AD 100 or at the latest 150, Christians had come to a consensus that the distinguishing marker of Christian life and worship was Sunday and that Sabbath observance was to be left behind with the many other Jewish festivals also listed in the Scriptures. But this was never a Christian reinterpretation of the Sabbath. It was instead a different celebration that superseded what the Sabbath offered.

This approach to the Sabbath parallels what Christians thought about the Day of Atonement or even Passover. The coming of Christ and his saving work of crucifixion-resurrection was like new wine in old wineskins. *And the old wineskins could not survive this new turn of events.* Christ had made obsolete many of the former rituals, and he revised many others by his coming. For the earliest Christians, to revive the ancient Jewish festivals would be tantamount to denying the epoch-changing significance of the gospel itself.

A WINESKIN

FAITH AND THE JEWISH FESTIVALS

I recently met with a friend who pastors a large evangelical church in the Midwest. He had recently preached on John 6 and in his sermons explained all about the Jewish Feast of Passover. His congregation was fascinated. It didn't take long before many were approaching him asking why their congregation didn't celebrate the Passover every year. "It would be biblical," they argued. "Since Jesus celebrated Passover maybe we should too."

This is not a new discussion. Christians have frequently argued for retaining many of the Jewish festivals in the church. Today the Messianic Jewish community has creatively sought to revive these festivals and bring them to "fulfillment" by showing the way that they point to Christ. And this may be one satisfying option. Here the Passover (with its fullest use of Jewish culture) could be celebrated, Christ's last meal and death applied to it, and the deeper meaning of the sacrifice of a lamb (for us: the Lamb being Christ) made plain. I have attended many of these services, and they have been wonderful in every respect.

In 1 Corinthians 5:7 Paul refers to Christ as our "Passover lamb [Gk. *pascha*]," and this may indicate he is thinking along these lines. But we have no evidence of New Testament believers *Christianizing* the Jewish festivals. Yes, Paul marks time by referring to them (Acts 12:3–4; 20:6, 16; 27:9; 1 Cor. 16:8).[28] Or he may refer to them as a metaphor (such as the leaven of Passover, 1 Cor. 5:8). He may be celebrating them *as a believer in Christ*, but we can only speculate. Certainly there were other Jewish Christians who saw the keeping of the law and these festivals as important to them (Acts 21:20), and this became a matter of some division within the church (Acts 21:17–26).

In a few of Paul's Gentile churches these ancient festivals and dietary customs were sometimes imposed on new believers, and their faith was judged by their use of them. In Colossians 2:16 Paul objects to this: "Therefore do not let anyone judge you by what you eat or drink, or with regard to a religious festival, a New Moon celebration or a Sabbath day." Why? Because these customs are a mere "shadow" of the reality that belongs to Christ (Col. 5:17; Heb. 8:5; 10:1). When Paul returned to Jerusalem after his third missionary tour, it may have been this sort of teaching that led some to criticize him in Jerusalem. Rumors flew: "They have been informed that you teach all the Jews who live among the Gentiles to turn away from Moses, telling them not to circumcise their children or live according to our customs" (Acts 21:21). Clearly the early Christians were working out what to do with these traditions. It may be fair to assume that whatever option they chose, a Jewish festival without reference to Christ was not among them.

The Jewish festivals provide us with background for understanding God's program for his people, but they do not necessarily serve as a vehicle of worship for the church. Passover commemorates the singular event of Jewish salvation: the exodus from Egypt. Christians do not find their salvation there but rather in Christ's death on the cross. Passover helps us understand his death, but as a festival it does not lead us to his death; Passover leads us to the exodus. However, as the New Testament believers "remembered" the Paschal events of bread and wine and sacrifice in obedience to Christ's command — during Passover — they eventually framed their own festival of sacrifice — the Eucharist or Lord's Supper — in which the Passover and its immediately applicable elements were used to interpret the cross.

We hold Judaism in highest respect. We admire their festivals. And in the church we study them and build a genuine *continuity* between Old Testament faith and our Christian faith. But there is also significant *discontinuity*. What happened in Christ shifted the way in which God's people understand his activity in the world. The coming of Christ was not a tremor but an earthquake of epic proportions that left no building standing. Everything would have to be rebuilt in light of what had transpired in Christ.

Therefore it has often been the judgment of the church—consistent throughout history—that Christians embrace their own festal markers that announce the gospel in worship. And when they use the Jewish festivals (as we see among modern Messianic Christians), the changes affected by Christ must always be present. Passover provides us with how we frame what we do, but it is the gospel that gives it its meaning.

Thus we do not worship God with a Passover Meal; we worship him with the Lord's Supper (or Eucharist) that is anchored to Passover but moves beyond it definitively. We do not celebrate an Egyptian lamb that was slain to protect God's people; rather, we announce the Lamb of God who takes away the sins of the world.

NOTES

1. www.marshmallowpeeps.com/
2. Cited in E. P. Sanders, *Judaism: Practice and Belief. 63 BCE—66 CE* (Philadelphia: Trinity International, 1992), 119.
3. This is when shoppers hit the stores on the day after Thanksgiving and shop ledgers move from "red" (debit) to "black" (profit).
4. Marva Dawn, *Keeping the Sabbath Wholly: Ceasing, Resting, Embracing, Feasting* (Grand Rapids: Eerdmans, 1989).
5. S. Safrai, "Religion in Everyday Life," in S. Safrai and M. Stern, eds., *The Jewish People in the First Century*, 2 vols. (Philadelphia: Fortress, 1976), 2:807. Safrai refers to Tertullian's *Ad Nationes* Bk 1, Ch 13, who defends Christianity before pagans by noting the many ways they imitate foreign religions such as Judaism; see Josephus, *Ag. Ap.* 2.282; *War* 7.45; 2.560. Compare the Roman centurion Cornelius as recorded in Acts 10:2.
6. Sanders, *Judaism: Practice and Belief*, 209.
7. This rabbinic text is cited in Gale A. Yee, *Jewish Feasts and the Gospel of John* (Wilmington, DE: Michael Glazier, 1989), 38–39.
8. See www.abu.nb.ca/Courses/NTIntro/LifeJ/PDFReadings/MishnahShabb.pdf.
9. Notice that John 5:4 is not in many recent Bible translations but instead is in the footnote. The oldest and best Greek manuscripts we possess today do not record the superstition about the angels. But at least some scribes who knew the story decided to insert it into John's gospel. Today we know that John did not write this. But it still means that this explanation was circulating quite early.
10. Many scholars place the Passover assembly at 300,000 (Sanders, *Judaism: Practice and Belief*, 132–38), but this is considered by most to be excessive.
11. Safrai and Stern, eds., *The Jewish People in the First Century*, 2:808–10.
12. For many scholars, this announcement echos another theme from Passover. "It is I" is actually the Greek version of the Hebrew name of God given to Moses on Mount Sinai (Ex. 3:6).
13. Jared Diamond, *Guns, Germs, and Steel: The Fates of Human Society* (New York: Norton, 1997), 141.
14. Michael Homan, "Did the Ancient Israelites Drink Beer?" *Biblical Archaeology Review* 36/5 (Sept/Oct 2010): 49–56.
15. Josephus, *J.W.* 6.301; cited in Sanders, *Judaism: Practice and Belief*, 141.

16. This is taken from H. Danby, *The Mishnah: Translated from the Hebrew with an Introduction and Brief Explanatory Notes* (Oxford: Oxford Univ. Press, 1933), 180.

17. See Tosefta, *Sukkah* 3:11–12. Cited in Yee, *Jewish Feasts in the Gospel of John*, 75.

18. Stan Guthrie, "The Blessings of Gratitude," *Christianity Today Online* (Nov. 24, 2010). See his book, *All That Jesus Asks* (Grand Rapids: Baker, 2010).

19. The tradition is found in the Babylonian Talmud, *Shabbat* 2: "What is Hanukah? The rabbis taught: 'On the twenty-fifth day of Kislev Hanukkah commences and lasts eight days, on which lamenting (in commemoration of the dead) and fasting are prohibited. When the Hellenists entered the sanctuary, they defiled all the oil that was found there. When the government of the House of Hasmoneans prevailed and conquered them, oil was sought (to feed the holy lamp in the sanctuary) and only one vial was found with the seal of the high priest intact. The vial contained sufficient oil for one day only, but a miracle occurred, and it fed the holy lamp eight days in succession. These eight days were the following year established as days of good cheer, on which psalms of praise and acknowledgment (of God's wonders) were to be recited.'"

20. For more on the techniques of ancient shepherding, see Gary M. Burge, *The Bible and the Land* (Grand Rapids: Zondervan, 2009), 49–58.

21. Scholars reading this reconstruction will at once recognize that I have made an important narrative move in this story. Some believe that John's account places the meal on the evening of Nisan 14, thereby letting Jesus be crucified the next day when the lambs are slain. This is taken from John 19:14, 31, and 42, which refer to the day of crucifixion as "the day of preparation for the Sabbath." By this account, Jesus' meal was not his Passover. However, other scholars disagree. We have no record of Judaism ever describing Nisan 14 as a Day of Preparation. The "preparation" that John is pointing to is preparation for the Sabbath, which 19:31 makes clear. They bury Jesus quickly (19:42) not because they must prepare for Passover but because Sabbath is near and no work may be done. This result aligns the Synoptics with John and suggests a translation in John 19:14: "It was the day of Sabbath preparation during Passover." The chief difficulty with this view is in 18:28. A defense of this position is available in my own commentary (*John*, NIV Application commentary [Grand Rapids: Zondervan, 2000], 364–67); and Craig Blomberg, *The Historical Reliability of the Gospels* (Downers Grove, IL: InterVarsity Press, 1987), 175–80.

22. There are, of course, competing interpretations of the meaning of the lamb referred to in John 1:29. But this is not the place to debate them. The majority view interprets John's comment as referring to the Passover sacrifice.

23. For the range of interpretations, see Craig Keener, *The Gospel of John* (Peabody, MA: Hendrickson, 2003), 2:1151–54.

24. *Exodus Rabbah* 122a and Targum Onkelos on Num. 20:11 (cited frequently in major commentaries).

25. References are from B. Chilton, "Festivals and Holy Days: Jewish," in Craig A. Evans, Stanley E. Porter, *Dictionary of New Testament Background* (Downers Grove, IL: InterVarsity Press, 2000), 373–74.

26. The connection between the Jewish Pentecost and the story in Acts 2 is disputed by some New Testament scholars. If the development of the Jewish link between Pentecost and covenant renewal is late (after the NT era), then the link cannot be made.

27. The precise use of the *Birkat Haminim* (which means "blessings on the heretics") is disputed among scholars. Most believe that it was used sometime after AD 80 and its chief aim was to flush out Jewish Christians who claimed an allegiance to Jesus as the Messiah and yet wanted to remain in the synagogue. In Jewish manuscripts found in Cairo (the Cairo Genizah) this "blessing" is not on heretics (*minim*) but on "Nazarenes" (i.e., the followers of Jesus).

28. In Acts 18:21 a minority of Greek manuscripts (represented in the KJV and the NKJV) show Paul saying: "I must by all means keep this coming feast in Jerusalem," but today the majority of scholars reject the sentence as an addition.

Share Your Thoughts

With the Author: Your comments will be forwarded to
the author when you send them to *zauthor@zondervan.com*.

With Zondervan: Submit your review of this book
by writing to *zreview@zondervan.com*.

Free Online Resources at
www.zondervan.com

Zondervan AuthorTracker: Be notified whenever your favorite authors publish new books, go on tour, or post an update about what's happening in their lives at www.zondervan.com/authortracker.

Daily Bible Verses and Devotions: Enrich your life with daily Bible verses or devotions that help you start every morning focused on God. Visit www.zondervan.com/newsletters.

Free Email Publications: Sign up for newsletters on Christian living, academic resources, church ministry, fiction, children's resources, and more. Visit www.zondervan.com/newsletters.

Zondervan Bible Search: Find and compare Bible passages in a variety of translations at www.zondervanbiblesearch.com.

Other Benefits: Register to receive online benefits like coupons and special offers, or to participate in research.